SWU-800- 004

UNIFORMS OF RUSSIAN ARMY DURING THE YEARS 1825-1855 VOL. 4

UNDER THE REIGN OF NICHOLAS I
EMPEROR OF RUSSIA BETWEEN 1825 TO 1855
GENDARMES, TRAIN, FOOT ARTILLERY, HORSE ARTILLERY
SAPPERS AND HORSE PIONEERS

From the Viskovatov's greatest work:
"Historical description of the clothing and
arms of the Russian Army"

English translation by Mark Conrad

SOLDIERSHOP PUBLISHING

AUTHOR

Aleksandr Vasilevich Viskovatov born 22 April (4 May New Style) 1804, died 27 February (11 March) 1858 in St. Petersburg, Russian military historian. He graduated from the 1st Cadet Corps and served in the artillery, the hydrographic depot of the Naval Ministry, and then in the Department of Military Educational Institutions. He mainly studied historical artifacts and the histories of military units. Viskovatov's greatest work was the Historical Description of the Clothing and Arms of the Russian Army.

Title: **UNIFORMS OF RUSSIAN ARMY DURING THE YEARS 1825-1855. VOL. 4** - **Under the reign of Nicholas I emperor of Russia between 1825-1855**
By A.V.Viskovatov. Serie edit by Luca S. Cristini. First edition by Soldiershop. July 2017
Cover & Art Design: Luca S. Cristini. Plates re-colorations by Anna Cristini. DTP Francesca Mangano
ISBN code: 978-88-93272629
Published by Soldiershop publishing, via Padre Davide, 7 - 24050 Zanica (BG) ITALY. www.soldiershop.com

UNIFORMS
OF THE RUSSIAN ARMY
DURING THE YEARS
1825-1855
VOL. 4

UNDER THE REIGN OF NICHOLAS I EMPEROUR OF
RUSSIA BETWEEN 1825 AND 1855

Nicholas I of Russia and Alexander Nikolayevich in 1854 by Bogdan Villevalde,

HISTORICAL DESCRIPTION OF THE CLOTHING AND ARMS
OF THE RUSSIAN ARMY - A.V. VISKOVATOV
(First English translation by Mark Conrad)

Soldiershop is glad to presents the complete collection of the great job made by A.V. Viskovatov dedicated to the uniforms and weapons belonging from the first Zar and Russian emperors to the Russian army during the Napoleonic period, until 1860 about. The time we considered in this volume corresponds to the reigns of Catherine the Great (Catherine II) who reigned since 1762 until his murder on the 6 November 1796.

Our reprint in based on the original 19th century volumes, to be precise the volumes from 4 to 6 are dedicated to the reign of Catherine II; this part is distributed on 3 or 4 volumes.

Our new edition, the first ever published in English, both on paper and digital format, boasts a large number of color plates, many of them unpublished and re-coloured by our team of expert artists and scholars of uniformology. Each volume is based on 100 color plates or more, always accompanied by the original translated text which describes the subjets of the plates.

A unique work in its genre, a must have in any respecting collection!

Aleksandr Vasilevich Viskovatov born 22 April (4 May New Style) 1804, died 27 February (11 March) 1858 in St. Petersburg, Russian military historian. He graduated from the 1st Cadet Corps and served in the artillery, the hydrographic depot of the Naval Ministry, and then in the Department of Military Educational Institutions.

He mainly studied historical artifacts and the histories of military units. Viskovatov's greatest work was the Historical Description of the Clothing and Arms of the Russian Army (Vols. 1-30, St. Petersburg, 1841-62; 2nd ed. Vols. 1-34, St. Petersburg - Novosibirsk - Leningrad, 1899-1948). This work is based on a great quantity of archival documents and contains four thousand colored illustrations.

Viskovatov was the author of Chronicles of the Russian Army (Books 1-20, St. Petersburg, 1834-42) and Chronicles of the Russian Imperial Army (Parts 1-7, St. Petersburg, 1852). He collected valuable material on the history of the Russian navy which went into A Short Overview of Russian Naval Campaigns and General Voyages to the End of the XVII Century (St. Petersburg, 1864; 2nd edition Moscow, 1946). Together with A.I. Mikhailovskii-Danilevskii he helped prepare and create the Military Gallery in the Winter Palace.

He wrote the historical military inscriptions for the walls of the Hall of St. George in the Great Palace of the Kremlin. (From the article in the Soviet Military Encyclopedia.)

CONTENTS

*

Preface pag. 5

*

*

HISTORICAL DESCRIPTION OF THE CLOTHING AND ARMS OF THE RUSSIAN ARMY
Gendarmes, Train, Foot Artillery, Horse Artillery, Sappers, and Horse-Pioneers 1825-1855

CHANGES IN THE UNIFORM AND ARMS OF THE ARMY FROM 20 NOVEMBER, 1825, TO 18 FEBRUARY, 1855:

11 – CORPS OF GENDARMES (*KORPUS ZHANDARMOV*).

12 April 1826 - The white **pants** [*pantalony*] with high boots and the grey **breeches** [*reituzy*] with stripes are withdrawn in the Gendarme Regiment [*Zhandarmskii polk*], the St.-Petersburg and Moscow Gendarme Battalions [*S.-Peterburgskii i Moskovskii Zhandarmskie diviziony*], and all Gendarme Commands [*Zhandarmskiya komandy*]. It is directed that grey breeches with red piping in the regiment and yellow piping in the battalions and commands be always worn (Illus. 364, 365, 366, and 367) [1].

15 September 1826 - Lower ranks who have served out the stipulated number of years and who voluntarily remain in service are directed to sew **gold galloon** [*nashivku iz zolotago galuna*] on the left sleeve, as described above for Cuirassier regiments [2].

30 December 1826 - Broadswords [*palashi*] are replaced with dragoon model **sabers** [*sabli*] in the Gendarme Regiment, the St.-Petersburg and Moscow battalions, and the Gendarme commands. At the same time both battalions receive the same coat [*mundir*] as the regiment, with red piping but, as before, without aiguillettes [*akselbanty*] (Illus. 368) [3].

1 January 1827 - It is directed that small forged and stamped stars [*kovanyya zvezdochki*] be worn on officers' **epaulettes** [*epolety*] to distinguish rank, in the same manner and arrangement as described above for Grenadier reg. [4].

27 April 1827 - In conjunction with the establishment of the **Corps of Gendarmes** [*Korpus Zhandarmov*] and its division into districts [*okrugi*], generals and officers of the corps are prescribed the same uniform as the Gendarme Regiment, but with hats cocked fore-and-aft [*shlyapy, nosit s polya*] (Illus. 369) [5].

9 May 1827 - The Gendarme Regiment, along with the Gendarme battalions and the commands, are given a new model of **helmet** [*kaska*] , the same as that established at this same time for Army Cuirassier regiments [6].

19 June 1827 - Gendarme generals, field-grade officers, and company-grade officers are directed to wear **frock coats** [*syurtuki*] and **greatcoats** [*shineli*] of light-blue cloth [*svetlosinyago sukna*]. The commands are to have yellow piping and, on the greatcoat collar, a yellow patch [*klapan*]. All others have red piping and red patches [7].

14 December 1827 - The **chevrons** [*nashivki*] instituted on 15 September 1826 for the left sleeves of lower ranks are directed to be of silver non-commissioned officers' lace [8].

24 March 1828 - Lower ranks are forbidden to have cinches in their **coats** [*mundiry*] [9].

26 December 1829 - All ranks of the Gendarme Regiment and the Gendarme battalions are directed to have uniform **buttons** with a raised image of a single-flame grenade [10].

8 June 1832 - Generals, field-grade officers, and company-grade officers are permitted to wear **moustaches** [11].

19 August 1832 - The **Warsaw Gendarme Battalion** [*Varshavskii Zhandarmskii divizion*], established in Warsaw, is to wear the same uniform as the St.-Petersburg and Moscow battalions [12].

15 April 1834 - **Cartridge pouches** [*lyadunki*] and **belts** are to be according to the new model, with a smaller sized cover and narrower belt [13].

2 May 1834 - In order to permit a better handling of the **sabers**, their hilts are to be redone in the new style as described above for Dragoon regiments [14].

4 February 1835 - A new model **helmet** is established for all Gendarmes, being lower than before and the same as that introduced at this same time for Cuirassier regiments [15].

28 February 1835 - Every non-commissioned officer and private [*ryadovoi*] of the Gendarme Regiment, the St.-Petersburg, Moscow, and Warsaw Gendarme battalions, and all Gendarme commands, are directed to have one **pistol** each, in a holster [*v chushke*] [16].

27 March 1835 - Lower ranks of the Gendarme Regiment, the Gendarme battalions, and the Gendarme commands are ordered to carry the **musket** [*ruzhe*] in the right hand when on foot, according to the example of the Life-Guards Horse-Grenadier Regiment. When mounted, the musket is carried in the small muzzle-bucket [*bushmat*] as before (Illus. 370) [17].

11 August 1835 - Gendarme non-commissioned officers are to have **muskets** [*ruzhya*] like the privates' [18].

31 January 1836 - Instead of ten buttons on the lower ranks' **greatcoats**, it is directed that there only be nine, as indicated above for Grenadier regiments [19].

1 July 1836 - Upon the separation of the **Gendarme commands** from the Internal Guard [*Vnutrennaya Strazha*] and their transfer to the Corps of Gendarmes, the yellow on their uniforms and saddle cloths [*valtrapy*] is replaced with red (Illus. 370) [20].

9 October 1836 - Staff-trumpeters and trumpeters [*Shtab-trubachi i trubachi*] are to have their **pistols** in a special model holster [*chushka*] attached to the left side of the saddle on top of the saddle cloth. They are to have a cartridge pouch and belt for their cartridges like that of the other lower ranks [21].

17 January 1837 - The rules for wearing the **saber** with the frock coat, as described above for Dragoon regiments, are confirmed [22].

15 July 1837 - The new form of officers' **sash** [*sharf*], the same as that described above for Grenadier regiments, is confirmed [23].

21 September 1837 - It is ordered that the Gendarme Regiment have **swordknots** [*temlyaki*] with leather tassels like those of other cavalry regiments, instead of wool tassels [24].

17 December 1837 - The new model of officers' **epaulettes**, identical to that introduced at this same time in Cuirassier regiments, which is to say with a fourth twist of cord, is confirmed [25].

4 January 1839 - Generals and officers are not to have bows or bands [*banty*] on their **pants**, but are rather to wear them completely flat [*gladkii*] in the style stipulated for lower ranks [26].

16 October 1840 - The regulation for silver **chevrons** [*shevrony*] for lower ranks, as described above for Grenadier regiments, is confirmed [27].

23 January 1841 - The capes [*bolshie vorotniki*] of officers' **greatcoats** are to have a length, measured from the lower edge of the collar [*malyi vorotnik*], of one arshin [28 inches] [28].

8 April 1843 - Those lower rank gendarmes with **aiguillettes** are directed to have them without knots [*uzly*] between the buttonhole and the metal endpoint. At the same time, the lower ranks of the Gendarme battalions and commands are to have the same **swordknots** as the Gendarme Regiment, i.e. all leather. On this same date are established stripes sewn onto **epaulettes** and **shoulder straps** for distinguishing rank, the same as described above for Dragoon regiments except with silver galloon instead of gold (Illus. 371) [29].

2 January 1844 - Officers are to have a **cockade** [*kokarda*] on the band of their forage caps, as described above for Grenadier regiments [30].

20 May 1844 - The new listing of differences among lower ranks' **forage caps** [*furazhnyya shapki*] is confirmed. On this basis, they are light-blue as before, but the piping on the top is to be red for the 1st Battalion [*divizion*] of the Gendarme Regiment, white for the 2nd, dark-blue for the 3rd, and red for the St.-Petersburg, Moscow, and Warsaw battalions and all commands. The cap band is light blue with red piping around both the upper and lower edges, with cut-out figures backed by yellow cloth [*prosechnyi, na zheltom sukne*], these being the squadron number and the Cyrillic letter "E" [for *eskadron* — M.C.] for the Gendarme Regiment and the capital battalions, and for the commands the first letter of their name and the Cyrillic letter "K" [for *komanda* — M.C.]. Colors for officers are the same as for the lower ranks, but without numbers or letters on the cap bands [31].

21 September 1844 - In the Gendarme Regiment the **standard-bearer non-commissioned officers** [*shtandartnye unter-ofitsery*] are directed to always wear the cartridge pouch under the standard crossbelt [*shtandartnaya perevyaz*] when in formation [32].

27 January 1845 - The former **helmets** with horsehair plumes [*plyumazh*] are replaced with new ones with hanging plumes [*sultany*], in the same style as that introduced at this same time for Cuirassier regiments. The hanging horsehair plumes are white in the Gendarme Regiment, black in the Gendarme battalions and commands (Illus. 372), and red for all trumpeters (Illus. 373). Henceforth only generals are left with hats [33].

5 February 1845 - Field and company-grade officers who are not attached to the regiment, battalions, or commands, but are part of the Corps of Gendarmes and who wear aiguillettes, are directed to have **helmets** with a white horsehair plume [34].

7 October 1847 - Upon the introduction of **drummers** [*barabanshchiki*] into the organization of the Gendarme Regiment, they are prescribed the same uniform as stipulated for trumpeters of the regiment (Illus. 373) [35].

9 January 1848 - Field and company-grade officers, on those days when after being relieved [*posle razvoda*] they are obliged to remain in holiday uniform [*prazdnichnaya forma*], are allowed to wear **frock coats**, **pants**, and **helmets** with plumes when walking out [36].

25 April 1848 - Valises [*chemodany*] are no longer to have flaps with buttons [37].

24 December 1849 - **Gold sabers** awarded "*Za khrabost*" ["For courage"] are to have a gilded grip on the hilt [38].

30 March 1851 - The **cartridge-pouch belt** is to be one 1 3/4 inches wide, with the previous small cap pouch [*kapsyulnaya sumochka*] [39].

24 January 1853 - Combatant lower ranks of Gendarme commands of the **Caucasus Territory** [*Kavkazskii krai*] are given a new uniform as follows:

a.) **Sheepskin hat** [*Shapka (papakha)*] — of black ram's fleece, with the top of light-blue cloth with red cloth piping, of the same pattern throughout as that established for lower ranks in the Caucasus.

b.) **Half-caftan** [*Polukaftan*] - light-blue cloth with the same color collar and cuffs, with red piping on the collar, cuffs, front of the half-caftan, and pocket flaps, of the same pattern throughout as the half-caftan of the troops of the Caucasus Corps. There are 15 buttons, of which 9 are on the front, 2 at the waist, 2 on the pocket flaps, and 2 on the epaulettes; 4 pairs of iron hooks are sewn to the collar; the skirts of the polukaftan, as in the Caucasus Corps, have no hooks. Non-commissioned officers have silver galloon on the collar and cuffs.

c.) **Epaulettes** — as before.

d.) *Sharavary* [wide Caucasian pants] — of greyish light-blue cloth, with a red stripe, of the same pattern throughout as the sharavary of lower ranks of the Caucasus Corps but lined with leather at the foot and having the same straps as cavalry trousers; instead of tinned buttons, 14 bone buttons are prescribed.

e.) **Gloves** — chamois, without gauntlets [*bez krag*].

f.) *Shashka* [Caucasian sword] — dragoon model.

g.) **Swordbelt over the shoulder** — chamois [*losinnaya*] with brass fittings, of the dragoon pattern.

h.) **Cartridge pouch with belt and firing cap pouch** — of the former pattern (Illus. 374).

Non-combatant personnel are prescribed a uniform like that of non-combatants of the Caucasus Corps, that is, shapka hat (papakha) instead of forage cap, half-caftan instead of frock coat or jacket [*kurtka*], and sharavary trousers (of the same color as previously) instead of pants [40].

31 January 1853 - Officers of those commands in, and in general all those officers under, **District VI of the Corps of Gendarmes** [*VI-i Okrug Korpusa Zhandarmov*], with the exception of the Astrakhan Command for which the present changes do not apply, are directed to have:

1.) The shapka instead of the helmet, like that issued to the Separate Caucasus Corps. The top of the shapka is of sky-blue cloth lined with silver lace which has two narrow, single-thread lines down the middle.

2.) A parade half-caftan [*paradnyi polukaftan*] of sky-blue cloth instead of the coat [*mundir*]. Collar and cuffs of the same color as the half-caftan with silver lace bars; red lining to the collar; red cloth piping on the collar, cuffs, and down the front to the bottom edge of the skirt and on the pocket flaps; lining the same color as the half-caftan; buttons, epaulettes and shoulder-straps, and aiguillettes (for those directly under the Corps of Gendarmes) are the same as on the coat.

3.) A vice-half-caftan [*vitse-polukaftan*] instead of the frock coat [*syurtuk*], similar throughout to the parade half-caftan but without the lace bars on the collar and cuffs.

4.) Sharavary trousers instead of pants, grey-blue cloth with red piping.

5.) Dragoon pattern saber instead of the cavalry pattern saber, with the appropriate sword-belt of silver lace. Spurs, swordknot, sash, greatcoat, forage cap, and horse furniture remain as before. Gloves are prescribed to be without gauntlets (Illus. 375) [*] [41].

(*Note: Civilian officials of the Directorate [*Upravlenie*] of the 6th District of the Corps of Gendarmes [*6-i Okrug Korpusa Zhandarmov*] have uniforms as follows: Secretaries and Translators - the same as for officials of Staffs and Directorates of places in the Caucasus subordinate to the War Ministry; Auditors [*Auditory* - a kind of military legal official] - the same as for Auditors of the Separate Caucasus Corps.)

13 August 1853 - Officers in campaign dress of **frock coat** without sash are directed to fasten the **swordbelt** over the frock [42].

18 February 1854 - The regulations established 15 November 1853 for light-cavalry **horse furniture**, and described above in the section for Army Cuirassier regiments, are extended to the Gendarmes [43].

29 April 1854 - Officers are directed to have campaign **greatcoats** [*pokhodnyya shineli*] of the same color and pattern as those of the lower ranks based on the instructions described above for Cuirassier regiments (Illus. 376) [44].

NOTES TO THE ILLUSTRATIONS
By Mark Conrad

364. The Gendarme Regiment was raised in 1815 by converting the Borisoglebsk Dragoons. Gendarme uniforms where what Russian call "light blue" but what we might think of as a medium shade of blue. Distinguishing colors were limited to piping (collar, cuffs, and turnbacks were blue like the uniform) which was red except at first for the Gendarme commands which for a time had yellow piping. Cuffs were as for dragoons, being round without any flap and with two buttons at the top edge. Buttons and appointments were silver, and the aiguillette was white worsted. White worsted epaulettes with a fringe replaced red shoulder straps for the Gendarme Regiment in 1817. The shabraque was blue with a wide band and a thin edge in white for the Gendarme Regiment, but with three thin stripes for the Gendarme battalions. The cartridge pouch had a round plate with a double-headed eagle. The forage cap was blue with three red pipings.

365. Officers' lace was silver, as was the aiguillette.

366. Trumpeters' lace was white, the trumpet brass, and the cords white.

367. The shoulder straps were red like the piping. NCO lace was silver.

371. Rank stripes are light colored over a darker base strap.

373. The shabraque is blue with three red lines of piping and a white monogram and crown edged in red. The trumpeter's swallow nests on his shoulders have a blue base with red piping at the bottom, all covered with white tape.

374. The monogram on the officer's shabraque was silver.

376. The great coat was blue with red piping on the collar along with a red tab. Lower ranks' shoulder straps were red.

12 - ARMY TRAIN (*ARMEISKII FURSHTAT*).

15 September 1826 - Lower ranks who have completed the regulation number of years of faultless service and voluntarily remain on active duty are to wear **gold galloon** sewn onto the left sleeve, as described above for Grenadier regiments [45].

1 January 1827 - Officers' **epaulettes** are to have small forged and stamped stars as rank distinctions in the same pattern and scheme as described above for Grenadier regiments [46].

13 October 1827 - Train officers [*Furshtatskie ofitsery*] are to have **epaulettes** with scales, like those introduced at this time for Dragoon, Horse-Jäger, Hussar, and Lancer regiments [47].

14 December 1827 - The **chevrons** [*nashivka*] sewn onto the left sleeve as established for lower ranks on 15 September 1826 are to be silver [48].

24 March 1828 - The **coats** of lower ranks are not to be tailored with cinches [49].

17 February 1829 - The Train [*Furshtat*, from German *Fuhrstaat* — M.C.] is to have the same **shako** [*kiver*] as issued to other troops, with the brigade number cut out on the shield on the shako plate, but with no cords [*etishkety*] for lower ranks (Illus. 377). Non-commissioned officers have cavalry-pattern **galloon**, and officers are to wear **moustaches** [50].

8 October 1829 - Lower ranks of Train battalions [*Furshtatskie bataliony*] are to have dark-blue pompons [*pompony*] on the **shako** (Illus. 378) [51].

26 December 1829 - Personnel of the Train in the Grenadier Corps are to have uniform **buttons** with the raised image of a grenade with the battalion number. Train personnel of the Lithuania have the Cyrillic letter L, while other corps have only the brigade number [52].

4 April 1830 - Officers are to have silver pompons on their **shakos** (Illus. 379) [53].

28 August 1830 - Directives concerning the uniform of the Train are as follows:

1st) All Train battalions are to have **shako plates** with the brigade number and dark-blue **shoulder straps** with the battalion number in yellow cloth.

2nd) Companies attached to **Infantry** regiments are to have piping around the shoulder strap [*vokrug pogonov*] as follows: 1st company — red, 2nd — white, 4th — green, 5th — green, on the lower edge of the shoulder strap right on the seam [*pod nizhnim kraem pogana u samago shva*], 6th — red, on the lower edge of the shoulder strap right on the seam. The 3rd company has no piping.

3rd) The Train attached to the **Artillery** has black piping around the shoulder strap.

4th) The Train attached to the **Cavalry** has piping in the regimental color, but in the color of the shako for Hussar regiments. In those cases when the piping would otherwise be light blue, the shoulder straps are to have no piping.

5th) The Train attached to the **Horse-Artillery** has black piping on the lower edge of the shoulder strap.

6th) The Train attached to **Sapper** battalions and **Pontoon** sections [*Pontonnyya otdeleniya*] has red piping, while those attached to **Corps and Division Headquarters** or who are in the Train that is directly part of Train companies have black piping. Both color pipings are on the upper edge of the shoulder strap where it fastens to the button [*po verkhnemyu krayu pogona, gde onyi zastegivaetsya na pugovitsu*] [54].

13 October 1831 - The newly-established Train of the **1st Horse-Pioneer Squadron** is to have the same uniform as the rest of the Train, but with red shoulder straps with the number 1 in yellow cloth. The shako plate is as for the combatant ranks of the squadron [55].

3 January 1833 - Covers for the **shakos** are abolished [56].

20 January 1833 - Covers for the **shakos** are to be as before [57].

28 January 1833 - Officers and Train lower ranks of Non-Combatant companies and detachments [*Nestroevya roty i otdeleniya*] in the **Grenadier Corps** and six **Infantry Corps** as well as in the **19th Infantry Division** are to have the Train uniform [*mundir*] with the number of the regiment to which the company is assigned on shakos and buttons and the number of the division to which they are attached on epaulettes and shoulder straps [58].

22 February 1833 - Train officers are not to use the hat [*shlyapa*], but are to always wear **shakos** [59].

21 March 1833 - Officers and Train lower ranks of Non-Combatant companies in the **Reserve Cavalry Corps** and **Light Cavalry Divisions** are prescribed the Train uniform [*mundir*], with the number of the regiment to which they are assigned on shakos and buttons and the number of the division to which they belong on epaulettes and shoulder straps [60].

5 May 1833 - The numbers on **shako plates** are not to be cut out, but made out of yellow brass and separately attached as described for the various regiments above [61].

28 December 1833 - Train lower ranks of Non-Combatant detachments in the **Field Artillery** [*Polevaya Artilleriya*] are prescribed the Train uniform, with the number of the Artillery brigade to which they are assigned on shakos, buttons, and epaulettes. Moreover, detachments in the **Caucasus Corps** are to replace the shako with the sheepskin headdress [*shapka*] prescribed on 10 August 1829 for the infantry of this corps [62].

15 March 1834 - Officers and lower ranks of Non-Combatant companies in the **Separate Caucasus Corps** are prescribed the Train uniform [*obmundirovanie*] based on the regulations confirmed on 28 January and 21 March of 1833 for Non-Combatant companies of other Army reg., except that the shako is replaced by the sheepskin shapka introduced in this corps on 10 August 1829 and described above for Army regiments (Illus. 380) [63].

2 May 1834 - For better handling, the hilts of the **sabers** are to be reworked in the new style as explained above for Dragoon regiments [64].

3 May 1834 - Train lower ranks with the **Artillery** are to have black shoulder straps with red piping instead of light-blue ones (Illus. 380) [65].

31 January 1836 - The lower ranks' **greatcoat** [*shinel*] is to have nine buttons instead of ten, as described above for Grenadier reg. [66].

27 April 1836 - The lower **pompons** [*repeiki*] are to be lined with black leather [67].

17 January 1837 - The directives for wearing the **saber** with the **frock coat** are approved as laid out above for Dragoon reg. [68].

15 July 1837 - Approval is given to a new pattern of officers' **sash**, identical to that described above for Grenadier reg. [69].

17 December 1837 - Approval is given to a new pattern of officers' **epaulettes**, identical to that described above for other regiments, i.e. with the addition of a fourth twist of braid [70].

4 January 1839 - Officers are not to have any bows or bands on the front of their **pants**. These are to be worn completely plain in the manner prescribed for lower ranks [71].

13 July 1839 - Officers of the Train in **Sapper** battalions are to have scaled epaulettes [*cheshuichatye epolety*] like those for Train officers of the infantry and cavalry [72].

15 July 1839 - Train privates assigned to **corps and divisional headquarters**, with the supply wagons [*proviantskiya telegi*] and the rest of the train [*oboz*], are to have plain buttons on their uniform clothing, a plain device on their shako plates, and shoulder straps in the Train color without any cut-out (Illus. 381) [73].

19 October 1840 - The regulation regarding **chevrons** [*shevrony*] for lower ranks is confirmed as laid out above for Grenadier regiments [74].

29 October 1840 - The Train in **Sapper** battalions is to have the Sapper insignia of two axes in addition to the number and letters on their buttons and shako plates [75].

23 January 1841 - The capes of officers' **greatcoats** are to be 28 inches long as measured from the lower edge of the collar [76].

1 June 1841 - Lower ranks in the Train attached to the **1st Rifle Battalion** are to have light-blue shoulder straps piped black on their coats and greatcoats. The number and letter 1.C. [Cyrillic S for *Strelkovyi* = Rifle] are to be on the shoulder straps, buttons, shako plates, and shako covers [77].

26 November 1842 - Until a new uniform is approved, officers and lower ranks of the Train in the **Separate Caucasus Corps** are to wear forage caps in place of the sheepskin shapka [78].

8 April 1843 - Train lower ranks are to have leather **sword-knots** with leather tassels. At this same time, stripes [*nashivki*] are sewn on the **shoulder strap** as a means of differentiating the lower ranks of the Train, based on the system described above for Army infantry except that silver galloon is used instead of gold. Concurrently, approval is given to a new pattern **shako** identical to the one established at this time for Grenadier, Infantry, and other regiments (Illus. 382) [79].

2 June 1843 - The manner of fitting the **shako plate** is confirmed as laid out above for Grenadier regiments [80].

29 November 1843 - Train lower ranks attached to **Mountain batteries** [*Gornyya batarei*] of the Separate Caucasus Corps are to be uniformed like the train personnel [*furleity*, from German *Fuhrleute* — M.C.] of the replacement parks [*zapasnye parki*], i.e. grey coats [*mundiry*] and similarly colored trousers [*reituzy*] and forage caps with visors. They are armed with short-swords [*tesaki*] and pistols just as the combatant [*stroevye*] personnel of these batteries [81].

2 January 1844 - Officers are to have a **cockade** on the band of their forage cap as described above for Grenadier reg. [82].

9 May 1844 - The Train is given **helmets** in place of shakos, identical with those approved on this same date for other troops, without plumes, and with the same plates as were on the shako (Illus. 383) [83].

20 May 1844 - Lower ranks of the entire Train are to have grey-colored **forage caps** with a light-blue band on which are cut out the company number and the Cyrillic letter *R* [for *rota* = company] in yellow cloth, and with light-blue piping around the top. Officers' forage caps are dark green with the band and piping in light blue, without any numbers or letters [84].

23 September 1844 - All Train non-commissioned officers are to have **saddles** without shabraques [*chepraki*], like the pattern approved for the same ranks in the Artillery [85].

4 January 1845 - Officers' **helmets** are to have, on the right side under the chin-scales, a cockade, as described above for Grenadier regiments (Illus. 384) [86].

19 May 1847 - Lower ranks of the Army Train are to have grey **forage caps** with a light-blue band, without any cut-out letters or numbers, and with light-blue piping around the top [87].

25 April 1848 - All flaps and buttons are removed from the **valises** [88].

8 August 1848 - Train personnel of the **Separate Caucasus Corps** are prescribed the new uniform and equipment approved at this time for the Grenadier regiments [89].

17 April 1852 - The alteration in the **water flask** and its manner of being carried, as established on 8 July 1851, is also applicable for Train lower ranks, with the only differences being that for them the flask is carried over the shoulder and that the flask strap is fitted with a buckle which allows the length of the strap to be adjusted to fit the stature of the soldier and the type of uniform he may be wearing (Illus. 385) [90].

13 August 1853 - Company-grade officers in the campaign uniform of **frock coat** without sash are to wear the **sword-belt** fastened over the frock coat [91].

18 February 1854 - The regulation of 15 November 1853 regarding light-cavalry **horse furniture** also applies to the Army Train [92].

29 April 1854 - In wartime, officers are to have campaign **greatcoats** according to the pattern established at this time for the Army and Guards, but with the collar and shoulder straps in light blue [93].

NOTES TO THE ILLUSTRATIONS
By Mark Conrad

377. The Train [*furshtat*] wore grey uniforms with "light-blue" facings and silver buttons. Forage caps were grey with a blue band. Swordknots varied according to the company as in the infantry. Non-commissioned officers had silver lace. Other ranks' pompons were blue. Officers' shako cords were silver. In 1819 it was ordered that shoulder straps have the corps number in yellow and be piped red in the first battalion of a brigade, white in the second, green in the third, and have no piping in the fourth. These pipings were repeated around the top of the forage cap. In 1820 the shoulder straps of the brigades attached to various corps were to be as follows: a Cyrillic G in the Grenadier Corps, 1K [for *Korpus* = Corps] in the 2nd and 3rd Reserve Cavalry Corps, 2K in the 4th and 5th Reserve Cavalry Corps, and a Cyrillic L in the Separate Lithuania Corps (this last also having raspberry piping on the collar and cuffs). For these brigades the previous pipings on the shoulder straps according to battalion were still valid.

378 and 379. The shabraque was grey with blue trim, and the crown and monogram were blue outlined in black. For officers, though, the crown and monogram were silver.

380. The greatcoat has a blue collar and shoulder straps as on the coat.

13 - FOOT ARTILLERY (*PESHAYA ARTILLERIYA*).

11 and 26 February 1826 - Officers and lower ranks of Foot Artillery, except for thosein the 24th and 25th Artillery Brigades of the Separate Lithuania Corps, are given single-breasted **coats** [*mundiry*] in place of the double-breasted ones, with nine flat buttons on the front, red cuff-flaps, and red piping down the front and from the bottom center to the turnbacks. In addition, officers have red piping on the pocket flaps and pleats. The former officers' grey riding trousers [*reituzy*] and pants [*pantalony*] with high boots and the lower ranks' pants with knee gaiters [*kragi*] are replaced with long, dark-green **pants** with red piping on the side seams. Lower ranks at all times, and company-grade officers only in formation and on parade, wear black cloth **half-gaiters** [*polushtiblety*] under these pants and over the boots, fastened with five or six small brass buttons (Illus. 386 and 387). Along with this change, the horizontal belt for the **knapsack** is to be between the two lower buttons on the front of the coat, while the **greatcoat** is carried on the knapsack rolled into a tube in its special oilskin case made of raven's-duck [*ravenduchnaya kleenka*] (Illus. 387). Generals, field-grade officers, and adjutants are to have boots with the **spurs** driven in [*pribivnye shpory*]. Companies of the **24th and 25th Brigades** receive the same pants, half-gaiters, and knapsacks as the companies of other brigades, but their coats continue to have plastrons (Illus. 388) [94].

10 May 1826 - Generals, field-grade officers, and those company-grade officers who are mounted when in formation [*v stroyu polozheno byt verkhom*], are during the summer to wear white linen **pants** [*polotnyanyya pantalony*] without integral spats [*kozyrki*], of the same pattern as previously described for the dark-green ones (Illus. 389). In addition, suede [*zamshevyya*] pants of the same pattern may be worn instead of the linen pants [95].

15 September 1826 - Lower ranks who have completed the regulation number of years of faultless service and have the right to be discharged but who voluntarily remain on active duty are to wear **gold galloon** [*nashivka iz zolotago galuna*] sewn onto the left sleeve above and in addition to the yellow tape [*bason*] prescribed on 29 March 1825 [96].

1 January 1827 - Officers' **epaulettes** are to have small forged and stamped silver stars as rank distinctions, without regard to monograms or letters, and of the same pattern and scheme as for the other troops of the army infantry and cavalry described above [97].

14 February 1827 - Pocket flaps [*karmannye klapany*] of officers' **coats** are not to have red piping [98].

23 March 1827 - Mounted helpers [*gandlangery*, from German *Handlanger* — M.C.], except for those in the Military Settlements [*Voennyya Poseleniya*], are to wear **riding-trousers** [*reituzy*] when mounted, and dark-green **trousers** [*bryuki*] with gaiters [*shtiblety*], or **summer pants** [*letniya pantalony*] during summer, when on foot [99].

31 July 1827 - Numbers and letters on the **covers** for shakos and pouches are changed from yellow cloth to yellow oil paint [100].

19 November 1827 - Highest Authority confirms that there is to be red cloth piping on the lower edge of the **collar** of coats and greatcoats [101].

24 March 1828 - The **coats** of lower ranks are not to be tailored with cinches [102].

24 April 1828 - Officers and lower ranks are given a new pattern **shako** [*kiver*], **shako plate** [*gerb*], and **badge for distinction** [*znak otlichiya*]. These are identical with those introduced at this time for regiments of Army infantry except for the lower part, or shield, of the shako plate. For companies in Grenadier brigades this has two crossed cannons and a single-flamed grenade engraved with the brigade number (Illus. 390 and 391), while for companies of field brigades this has the same two cannons without a grenade but with the number engraved above them (Illus. 392 and 393). Together with this there are the following changes:

1.) The width of the **crossbelt** and **swordbelt** [*perevyaz i portupeya*] is stipulated as 3 1/2 inches, of the **knapsack shoulder belts** [*rantsevye plechevye remni*] — 2 5/8 inches, and of the **belt across the chest** [*nagrudnyi remen*] — 2 inches.

2.) Knapsacks [*rantsy*] are to be of calfskin as before but with black leather trim. The knapsack is prescribed to be 15 3/4 inches by 4 3/8 inches in breadth and width, and 14 inches high. The length of the cover from the upper edge is 10 1/2 inches.

3.) In place of their grey coats [*mundiry*], all non-combatant non-commissioned officers are issued with dark-green **frock coats** [*syurtuki*] with a single row of buttons and the same collar, cuffs, and shoulder straps as for combatant personnel. **Pants**, however, are grey with red piping on the side seams (Illus. 394).

4.) Non-combatant craftsmen [*masterovye*] of the lower ranks, as well as medical orderlies [*lazaretnye sluzhiteli*] are to replace their coats with grey cloth **jackets** [*kurtki*] modeled on the coat. **Pants** are to be as for the non-combatants above (Illus. 394) [103].

28 July 1828 - In the **Rocket Company** [*Raketnaya rota*] officers' epaulettes and lower ranks shoulder straps are to have the letters *P. P.* (Cyrillic *R. R.*) [104].

10 November 1828 - The Army Foot Artillery (except the Grenadier brigades, which keep their plumes) is to have **pompons** [*pompony*] on the shako like those used by other troops, but made of red wool for lower ranks (Illus. 395) [105].

18 May 1829 - Non-commissioned officers who have been recommended by higher command for promotion to officer rank by virtue of years of service are to have **silver sword-knots** [106].

10 August 1829 - In the Artillery companies of the Separate Caucasus Corps the shako is replaced by a sheepskin *shapka* headdress like that introduced at this time for the Grenadier and Infantry regiments of this corps (Illus. 396) [107].

8 October 1829 - The shield on the shako plate in Artillery companies of the Separate Lithuania Corps is to have the Cyrillic letter *L.* on the grenade instead of a number, and in companies of the Caucasus Grenadier Artillery Brigade it is to have the letter *K.* [Cyrillic *K* for *Kavkazskaya* = Caucasus] instead of a number [108].

16 December 1829 - The black cuffs of officers' **frock coats** [*syurtuki*] are changed to dark green, with red piping as before (Illus. 397) [109].

26 December 1829 - All combatant ranks are to have **buttons** on coats, frock coats, and greatcoats with raised designs as follows:

a.) 1st, 2nd, and 3rd Grenadier Brigades — two crossed cannons and a single-flamed grenade with the brigade number (Illus. 398a).

b.) Grenadier companies of the Separate Lithuania Corps — the same cannons and grenade, but with the Cyrillic letter *L* instead of a number (Illus. 398b).

c.) Caucasus Artillery Brigade — the same cannons and a grenade with the letter *K* (Illus. 398c).

d.) Field brigades — the same cannons, but without a grenade, and with the brigade number (Illus. 398d) [110].

20 Aug 1830 - Officers' rapiers [*shpagi*] are replaced with **half-sabers** [*polusabli*] of the same pattern as that approved at this time for Grenadier and other regiments of Army infantry (Illus. 399) [111].

18 January 1831 - The **Rocket Company** is to have the same buttons as all the rest of the Field Artillery, but with the letters *1.P.* instead of a brigade number [112].

9 May 1831 - The companies of the 24th, 25th, and 26th Artillery Brigades of the **Separate Lithuania Corps** are to have the same uniform as the other companies of Field Artillery, i.e. without plastrons on the coat [113].

1 January 1832 - Generals who have the gold swords with diamonds inscribed "*za khrabost*" ["for courage"] are not to use sword-knots [114].

8 June 1832 - Officers are permitted to wear **moustaches** [115].

3 January 1833 - **Cloth half-gaiters** are abolished for company-grade officers and lower ranks (Illus. 400). Non-commissioned officers and lower ranks are no longer to use **covers** for their shakos and cartridge pouches. **Swordknots** are abolished for non-commissioned officers and privates except for those non-commissioned officers who have them in silver [116].

20 January 1833 - **Covers** for shakos are restored as before [117].

20 February 1833 - All combatant ranks are given new pattern **summer pants or trousers** [*letniya pantalony ili bryuki*], without buttons or integral spats (Illus. 401) [118].

22 February 1833 - Field and company-grade officers are not to use the hat, but rather use the **shako** at all times. Officers who must be mounted when in formation are permitted to have **horses** with long tails [119].

5 May 1833 - Instead of being cut out [*proreznyi*], the numbers on the **shako plates** are to be fixed on [*nakladnyi*], being made of tin for lower ranks and silver-plated for officers (Illus. 402 and 403) [120].

28 March 1834 - Highest Authority approves the new pattern for short-swords [*tesaki*] with yellow brass mountings and a straight blade (Illus. 404) [121].

26 April 1834 - **Numbers** and **letters** on shakos, covers, and forage caps are to be as follows: in the first battery companies [*pervyya batareinyya roty* - sic, actually all artillery companies had been retitled batteries by a statute of 28 December 1833 — M.C.] Cyrillic *1.B.*, the first light companies [*legkiya roty*] — Cyrillic *1.L.*, the first reserve companies [*rezervnyya roty*] — Cyrillic *1.R.*, the first park companies [*parochnyya roty*] — Cyrillic *1.P.*, and so on.

The upper piping on the **forage caps** in the first battery batteries [*batareinyya batarei* — here the correct words are used - M.C.] is red, in the second batteries — white, in the third batteries — dark blue, in the fourth batteries — light green, in the reserve batteries — yellow, and in the park batteries — dark green. In all these companies [sic] the upper and lower edges of the cap band are piped red, while the letter and number on the band are yellow [122].

13 May 1834 - Approval is given to the new model **saddle** and **shabraque** [*cheprak*] for the horses of mounted officers. The former are to be of black leather and the latter of dark-green cloth with black cloth stripes edged on both sides with red piping. Surcingles [*troki*] are to be striped black and red (Illus. 405) [123].

29 May 1834 - Under no circumstances are officers to wear **knapsacks** when in formation. They are at all times to wear **spurs** and have straps [*podmochki*] on the pants to pass under the sole of the boot [124].

15 July 1834 - Personnel of **Brigade Artillery Staffs** are to have the same uniform as prescribed for the batteries in accordance with the following:

1.) If only one battery in the brigade is entitled to badges for distinction of any kind, then the brigade personnel wear the uniform and distinctions of this battery.

2.) If several batteries in a brigade have badges for distinction, then the brigade personnel wear the uniform of that battery which has the most badges for distinction.

3.) If no battery in a brigade has any distinctions, then the brigade personnel have the uniform of the first heavy battery of that brigade [125].

26 September 1834 - Lower ranks are directed to wear the **knapsack** on two belts lying crosswise over the chest (Illus. 406) [126].

20 August 1835 - It is ordered that for lower ranks a linen case or pocket [*kholshchevyi chekhol, ili karman*] for the forage cap is to be put on the outside of **knapsack** on the side that lies on the soldier's back. These cases are to be made from the linings of worn-out coats. For drummers the knapsack is to have one belt as before, worn over the left shoulder [127].

31 January 1836 - The lower ranks' **greatcoat** [*shinel*] is to have nine buttons instead of ten, namely: six along the front opening, two on the shoulder straps, and one on the flaps behind [128].

27 April 1836 - **Lower pompons** [*repeiki*] are to be lined with black leather [129].

13 May 1836 - Girths [*podprugi*] for officers' **saddles** are to be dark green with red stripes [130].

21 October 1836 - Shako **plumes** [*sultany*] in the 1st, 2nd, and 3rd Grenadier Artillery Brigades are to be 19 1/4 inches high from the triangular socket [*tresovka*] to the top, with an upper circumference of 10 inches and a lower one of 7. Their weight is not to be more than 8 1/10 ounces [131].

14 January 1837 - The wooden parts of the handles of **entrenching tools** [*shantsovyi instrument*] are to be lacquered. The directives for the fitting and carrying of these tools are confirmed as laid out in detail above for Grenadier regiments [132].

15 July 1837 - The new pattern of officers' **sash** is approved, identical to that introduced at this time in the regiments of army infantry and cavalry and described above [133].

17 December 1837 - The new pattern of officers' **epaulette** is approved, identical with that introduced at this time in the regiments of army infantry and cavalry, i.e. with the addition of a fourth twist of braid [134].

4 January 1839 - Officers' **pants** and **trousers** are not to have any bows or bands on the front, but are to have them completely plain in the manner prescribed for lower ranks [135].

16 March 1839 - Lower ranks' **swordbelts** are to be 2 3/5 inches wide, while **drummers' crossbelts** are 4 2/5 inches wide as before [136].

16 October 1840 - Lower ranks who have earned the right to discharge on indefinite leave but who voluntarily remain on active service after completing the regulation term of service are to be given gold lace **chevrons** [*shevrony*] to be sewn onto the left sleeve, one for every five years of extra service, and which are to be worn during this subsequent service. On the same basis these same chevrons are to be given to non-commissioned officers who have declined promotion to officer rank and are receiving two-thirds of an ensign's pay for serving five or more years after declining such promotion [137].

23 January 1841 - The capes of officers' **greatcoats** are to be 28 inches long as measured from the lower edge of the collar [138].

26 November 1842 - Until a new uniform is approved, officers and lower ranks of the Artillery in the Separate Caucasus Corps are to wear **forage caps** in place of the sheepskin headdress [*shapka*] (Illus. 407 and 408) [139].

8 April 1843 - A new model **shako** is approved, curving slightly inward toward the bottom and with a plume identical to that confirmed at this time for Grenadier regiments (Illus. 409).

Rank distinctions for lower ranks in the form of trim [*nashivki*] sewn onto the shoulder straps of coats and greatcoats are established based on the scheme described for Grenadier and Infantry regiments: for fireworkers acting as sergeants [*feierverkery v dolzhnosti feldfebelei*][*] — as for sergeants, in gold galloon; for platoon fireworkers [*vzvodnye feierverkery*] — as for section non-commissioned officers [*otdelennye unter-ofitsery*]; for other fireworkers [*prochie feierverkery*] — as for junior non-commissioned officers [*mladshie unter-ofitsery*]; and for lance-corporals [*yefreitory*] — as for lance-corporals. For these last three grades the rank trim is white with a red stripe in the center for Grenadier brigades and all white for Field brigades, like the trim on the coats of musicians and drummers. Non-commissioned officers from the nobility [*unter-ofitsery iz dvoryan*] are given sewn-on gold galloon like the Army infantry, while lower ranks who return to their batteries from the Model Foot Artillery Battery or who are from the Instructional Artillery Brigade keep their yellow-tape trim [*nashivki iz zheltago basona*], as introduced in the Foot Artillery based on the system for Army infantry who have served in the Model Infantry or Instructional Carabinier Regiments.

On this same date it is directed that **drum-majors' epaulettes** [*tambur-mazhorskie epolety*] have red silk between the braided gold thread and in the hanging fringe so as to be more easily distinguished from epaulettes for field-grade officers (Illus. 410) [140].

[*Note: *Feierverker*, from German *Feuerwerker*. In the Russian artillery, non-commissioned officers were titled "fireworkers" in deference to their gunnery and artificer skills. Note also that here "non-commissioned officers" are what western armies would call sergeants, and "sergeants" are what would be called sergeants major - M.C.]

2 June 1843 - Approval is given to the manner of attaching the **shako plate** and **badge for distinction** in that the lower part of the plate, with or without the badge for distinction, covers half of the width of the lacquered shako strap. The cross on top of the crown in the plate would lie on the lower edge of the badge for distinction, while the badge for distinction itself would be even with the top of the shako (Illus. 410) [141].

29 November 1843 - Combatant lower ranks of the **Mountain Artillery** [*Gornaya Artilleriya*] of the Separate Caucasus Corps are to be armed with new-pattern short-swords [*tesaki*] and standard pistols [142].

2 January 1844 - Officers are to have a **cockade** on the cap band of the forage cap, identical with that introduced at this time in the regiments of Army infantry and cavalry and described above [143].

9 May 1844 - Shakos are replaced by **helmets** [*kaski*] identical to those established at this time for regiments of Army infantry. The 1st, 2nd, and 3rd Grenadier Brigades have black horsehair plumes [*sultany*] except for drum-majors, musicians, and drummers, who have red ones. The rest of the artillery have no plumes (Illus. 411 and 412). The artillery of the Caucasus Corps continues to wear forage caps [144].

20 May 1844 - Approval is given to a new scheme for differentiating the **forage caps** of the lower ranks. Based on this the piping around the upper part is red cloth while the cap band is black cloth with two red pipings, one on each edge, and has a cut-out battery number and letter backed by yellow cloth. Officers' cap bands are the same as for lower ranks but, as before, without numbers or letters [145].

4 January 1845 - Officers' **helmets** are to have, on the right side under the chin-scales, a cockade, as described above for Grenadier and other regiments of Army infantry (Illus. 413) [146].

The special statute ***Badges for distinction*** ["*Znaki otlichii*"] gives a detailed list of Foot Artillery batteries which have been awarded badges for distinction, to be worn on the shako and shapka headdress, and gold lace bars [*petlitsy*] for the collar and cuff-flaps of officers' coats, in accordance with the usage accepted during previous reigns. By 1 January 1846 these badges and lace bars were as follows:

a) Badges inscribed "*Za otlichie*" ["For excellence"] — Battery Battery №1 of the 1st Grenadier Artillery Brigade, Battery Battery №6 of the 3rd Grenadier Artillery Brigade, Battery Batteries №№1 and 2 of the 1st Artillery Brigade, Light Batteries №№3 and 5 of the 2nd Artillery Brigade, Battery Battery №4 and Light Battery №8 of the 3rd Artillery Brigade, Battery Battery №4 of the 6th Artillery Brigade, Light Battery №1 of the 7th Artillery Brigade, Battery Battery №3 and Light Battery №3 of the 8th Artillery Brigade, Battery Battery №1 of the 10th Artillery Brigade, Light Batteries №№4 and 5 of the 11th Artillery Brigade, Battery Battery № 4 of the 12th Artillery Brigade, Light Battery №5 of the 14th Artillery Brigade, Battery Batteries №№1 and 2 of the 16th Artillery Brigade, Battery Battery №4 and Light Battery №8 of the 18th Artillery Brigade, Battery Battery №1, Light Battery №2, and Mountain Battery №2 of the Caucasus Grenadier Artillery Brigade, Light Batteries №№3 and 5 of the 19th Artillery Brigade, and Mountain Battery №4 of the 20th Artillery Brigade.

b) Badges inscribed "*Za Varshavu 25 i 26 Avgusta 1831 goda*" ["For Warsaw 25 and 26 August of the year 1831"] — Battery Battery №2 of the 1st Grenadier Artillery Brigade, Battery Battery №5 of the 2nd Grenadier Artillery Brigade, Light Battery № 2 of the 1st Artillery Brigade, Battery Battery №3 of the 2nd Artillery Brigade, Light Batteries №№6 and 7 of the 3rd Artillery Brigade, Battery Battery №1 and Light Battery №1 of the 4th Artillery Brigade, Battery Battery №3 and Light Battery №4 of the 5th Artillery Brigade, Light Battery №6 of the 6th Artillery Brigade, and Light Battery №7 of the 9th Artillery Brigade.

c) Gold lace bars — Battery Batteries №№1 and 2 of the 1st Grenadier Artillery Brigade, Battery Battery №1 of the 1st Artillery Brigade, Battery Battery №4 of the 3rd Artillery Brigade, Battery Battery №1 of the 4th Artillery Brigade, Battery Battery №4 of the 6th Artillery Brigade, Battery Battery №3 and Light Battery №3 of the 8th Artillery Brigade, Battery Battery №2 of the 10th Artillery Brigade, Battery Battery №3 and Light Battery №4 of the 11th Artillery Brigade, Battery Battery №4 of the 12th Artillery Brigade, Battery Battery №4 and Light Battery №8 of the 18th Artillery Brigade, Battery Battery №1 and Mountain Batteries №№1 and 2 of the Caucasus Grenadier Artillery Brigade, and Battery

Battery №2 and Mountain Battery №4 of the 19th Artillery Brigade.

19 May 1847 - With the new, general directive concerning the colors for **forage caps** within the War Department [*Voennoe vedomstvo*, i.e. the entire army — M.C.], clerks [*pisarya*], medics [*feldshera*], and other lower ranks of the Foot Artillery with dark-green forage caps are to have cap bands and piping around the top part in the same colors as the cap bands and piping of combatant lower ranks. Barbers, hospital orderlies [*lazazretnye sluzhiteli*], and others with grey forage caps are to have piping on both edges of the cap band and around the top in the color of the facing cloth [147].

9 January 1848 - On those days when they are obliged to remain in ceremonial dress [*prazdnichnaya forma*] after the mounting of the guard [*posle razvoda*], field and company-grade officers of the 1st, 2nd, and 3rd Grenadier Artillery Brigades are permitted to wear the **frock coat** with **helmet** and plume for walking-out (Illus. 414) [148].

8 August 1848 - The Artillery of the **Separate Caucasus Corps** is prescribed the new uniform and equipment approved at this time for Grenadier regiments and described above (Illus. 415 and 416) [149].

16 September 1848 - In all Reserve and Replacement batteries [*Rezervnyya i Zapasnyya batarei*], lower ranks' **forage caps** are to have the Cyrillic letters *R.B.* or *Z.B.*, respectively [150].

31 October 1848 - Approval is given to the description of the officers' **swordbelt** and the manner of wearing both it and the slings of the half-saber, as related in detail above in the entry for Grenadier regiments for this same date [151].

24 November 1848 - The uniform changes of 8 August of this year are extended to also apply to **non-combatant personnel** [152].

14 September 1849 - The **percussion pistol** model for officers is approved, identical with that laid out above in the entry for Grenadier regiments [153].

9 November 1849 - **Helmets** are to be made lower than formerly so that when worn they cover the upper part of the ears [154].

25 November 1849 - The **sheepskin shapka**, confirmed on 8 August 1848 for infantry of the Separate Caucasus Corps and described above for Grenadier regiments, is to be worn somewhat toward the back of the head and tilted over the right brow so that the left side of the forehead is obliquely exposed [155].

24 December 1849 - The grip on the hilt of the **gold half-saber** awarded for bravery is to be gold instead of wrapped in black, lacquered leather [156].

28 May 1850 - It is directed that as a rule, when park artillery companies [*parkovyya artilleriiskiya roty*] are drawn up for inspection or formation, without their park equipment, on a battalion or company infantry basis, then the lower ranks are to have their **muskets** slung behind their backs as when in billets and hold their drawn **short-swords** in their hands. Muskets are to be carried in hand only when these companies are engaged in guard duties or are in formation with their park equipment [157].

17 January 1851 - Approval is given to the manner of gathering up and folding back the skirts of the **greatcoat** while on the march, as described in detail above for Grenadier regiments (Illus. 417) [158].

8 July 1851 - Approval is given to the **drum**, **fife case**, **water flask**, **greatcoat strap**, and **swordbelt** as described and laid out in detail above for Grenadier regiments (Illus. 418) [159].

20 October 1851 - The list and description of items to be carried by the soldier in his **knapsack** while on the march and during inspections is confirmed as laid out above for Grenadier regiments [160].

26 January 1852 - Non-combatant lower ranks with grey cloth **forage caps** are to have cloth cap bands of the same color as the collars of combatant personnel [161].

3 January 1853 - Non-combatant lower ranks with **frock coats** are to have these reach to the lower part of the knee [162].

18 February 1854 - The **saddles** of field and company-grade officers are to have, in back, a valise of light-blue cloth, of the pattern prescribed for cavalry officers. A greatcoat, rolled up according to the regulation established for cavalry troopers, is to be secured with small straps to the front arch above the saddle, in a leather case as related above for Grenadier regiments and other Army Infantry troops [163].

29 April 1854 - Generals and field and company-grade offices are to have campaign **greatcoats** in wartime, of the same pattern as established at this time for Grenadier regiments and worn according to the same guidelines [164].

16 June 1854 - The piping around the top of the **forage cap** is to be red in the newly-formed Grenadier Batteries №№7, 8, and 9 [165].

30 October 1854 - In the newly-established **Reserve Mobile Field Artillery Parks** [*Rezervnye Podvizhnye Polevye Artilleriiskie parki*] the shoulder straps of lower ranks, buttons, and small shield on the helmet plate are to have the figures *P. №1* [Cyrillic *R* for *Rezervnyi*] in Park №1 and *P. № 2* for Park №2 [166].

19 January 1855 - In the **Reserve Mobile Field Park** and **Reserve Field Flying Park** [*Rezervnye parki: Podvizhnyi Polevoi i Polevoi Letuchii*] which are intended to be formed, the shoulder straps of lower ranks, buttons, and the small shield on the helmet plate are to have the figures *P. № 3* in Park № 3 and *P. № 4* in Park № 4 [167]

386. Artillery uniforms were dark green with black cuffs, collar, and turnbacks, all piped red. Cuff flaps and shoulder straps were red, and buttons were brass or gold. Notice that the bombardier has gold non-commissioned officers' lace on the cuffs only, and not the collar. The shoulder straps has Cyrillic1 G for the 1st Grenadier Artillery Brigade. Shako cords were red (silver for officers).

388. The black plastron is piped red, and the red shoulder straps have a yellow 24.

389. The shabraque is dark green with two wide gold lace stripes near the edge. In this case white summer pants are worn.

390 and 392. The white pants with integral spats have white buttons.

394. The NCO's frock coat is dark green piped red, as is the forage cap. The other figure is entirely in grey piped red, including the forage cap. In both cases there is piping around the top of the cap and on both sides of the capband.

400. Dark-grey mittens are attached to the sword frog.

405. The shabraque is dark green with four red stripes. The color between the stripes is black.

415 and 416. The collar is black but the cuffs are dark green. Piping and shoulder straps are red. All equipment is black.

417. The collar of the greatcoat is black piped red, and shoulder straps are red with yellow lettering. This fireworker is wearing the white summer pants, as is the drummer in Illustration 418.

418. Drummers' and musicians' tape in the artillery was white.

14 -HORSE ARTILLERY (*KONNAYA ARTILLERYA*).

11 February 1826 - Clerks and in general all non-combatant lower ranks are to have grey **riding-trousers** [*reituzy*] with red stripes [*lampasy*] [168].

26 February 1826 - The entire Horse Artillery is to have red **cuffs** with three buttons on the cuff-flaps, as prescribed at this same time for the Foot Artillery (Illus. 419) [169].

15 September 1826 - Lower ranks who have completed the regulation number of years of faultless service but who voluntarily remain on active duty are to wear **gold galloon** sewn onto the left sleeve, as described in detail for Grenadier regiments [170].

21 October 1826 - The entire Horse Artillery, with the exception of that part in the 1st Lancer Division and the Lithuania Lancer Division, is to have only grey **riding-trousers** with red cloth piping on the side seams instead of the dark-green pants with stripes and the grey riding-trousers with stripes (Illus. 420) [171].

1 January 1827 - Officers' **epaulettes** are to have small forged and stamped stars as rank distinctions, without regard to monograms or letters, and of the same pattern and scheme as described above for regiments of Army Infantry and Cavalry [172].

26 February 1827 - Horse-Artillery companies in the 1st and Lithuania Lancer Divisions are to have, besides their present dark-green pants with red stripes, grey **riding-trousers** with red piping on the side seams, as prescribed for the rest of the Army Horse Artillery on 21 October 1826 [173].

31 July 1827 - The numbers and letters on **shako covers** are to be painted with yellow oil paints [174].

27 September 1827 - Saddle cloths [*valtrapy*] are to be edged round with red cloth piping (Illus. 421) [175].

8 October 1827 - A new pattern of **saber** [*sablya*] is approved, straighter than before and with a brass hilt [*yefes*], black grip [*grif*], and iron scabbard [*nozhny*] [176].

13 October 1827 - Combatant lower ranks are issued **scaled epaulettes** [*cheshuichatye epolety*] in the same color as their buttons, with a backing and strap of red cloth and the company numbers in white metal (Illus. 421). Together with this the field of the officers' epaulettes is also to be scaled and have a silver number (Illus. 421) [177].

19 November 1827 - Highest Authority confirms that the lower edge of the collar on coats and **greatcoats** has red cloth piping [178].

9 February 1828 - A new model **shako** is introduced for the entire Horse Artillery, identical with that established at this same time for Dragoon and Horse-Jäger regiments, but with the pompon and cords in red (silver for officers) (Illus. 422). The metal mountings on the shako remain as before (Illus. 423) [179].

20 December 1828 - New patterns for the **shako plate** and **badge for distinction** are confirmed based on those established on 24 April 1828 for the Foot Field Artillery, with the former having a cut-out figure of the battery number (Illus. 424) [180].

16 December 1829 - The black cuffs of officers' **frock coats** are changed to dark green, with red piping as before [181].

26 December 1829 - Uniform **buttons** are to have a raised representation of the same number as on the shako plate and two crossed cannons, like the design approved at this time for the companies of Foot Field Artillery brigades [182].

25 November 1830 - In the Horse-Artillery companies of the 1st and Lithuania Lancer Divisions, only officers are to keep the dark-green **pants** with red stripes [183].

6 May 1831 - **Horse-Artillery Companies №№5 and 6** in the 6th (formerly the Lithuania Lancer) Division are to have the same uniform as other Horse-Artillery companies, i.e. without plastrons [184].

26 December 1831 - The dark-green officers' **pants** in the just-mentioned companies are abolished [185].

3 January 1833 - **Shako covers** are abolished [186].

20 January 1833 - **Shako covers** are restored as before [187].

22 February 1833 - Field and company-grade officers are not to use the hat, but rather use the **shako** at all times [188].

16 March 1833 - The **undress coat** [*vitse-mundir*, literally "vice-mundir" — M.C.] of field and company-grade officers is abolished [189].

28 December 1833 - Instead of being cut out, the numbers on the **shako plates** are to be fixed on, being made of tin for lower ranks and silver-plated for officers, as introduced in the Foot Artillery (Illus. 425) [190].

13 April 1834 - Pouches and **pouch-belts** [*lyadunki i perevyazi*] are to be of the new pattern with a smaller cover and narrower belt [191].

26 April 1834 - **Numbers** and **letters** on the shakos, covers, and forage caps in Horse-Artillery batteries are to be as follows: in Heavy Battery №15 — Cyrillic *15.B.*, in Light Battery №1. — Cyrillic *1.L.*, in Reserve Battery №1 — Cyrillic *1.R.*, and so on. The upper piping of the **forage caps** is to be as before: red in Heavy batteries and white in Light batteries. The piping on the upper and lower edges of the cap band is red in all batteries, and in between are the same number and letter as prescribed for the shako cover [192].

2 May 1834 - For better handling, the hilts of the **sabers** are to be reworked in the new style as explained above for Dragoon regiments [193].

2 July 1834 - The lower ranks' leather **swordknots** with wool tassels are to be replaced with all-leather ones [194].

15 July 1834 - Personnel of the **headquarters** of Horse-Artillery brigades are to have uniforms in accordance with the guidelines confirmed at this same time for the Foot Artillery [195].

3 December 1834 - Throughout the entire Horse Artillery each man is to have a **pistol**, carried on his person in a special holster [*chushka*] (Illus. 425) [196].

7 December 1834 - When shakos are worn, the **shako lines** [*snury u kiverov*] are not to reach to the waist, but only halfway down the back [197].

4 January 1835 - Privates are to begin using **gloves** [*perchatki*] of greyish-blue cloth, made from worn-out riding-trousers. These are only to be worn at times when Infantry troops would be wearing their own cloth mittens [*rukavitsy*]. Non-commissioned officers keep their deerskin gloves [*losinnyya perchatki*] as before [198].

13 January 1835 - As a reinforcement to the order cited above for 3 December 1834, all mounted trumpeters, non-commissioned officers, and privates are directed to each have one **pistol** [199].

6 April 1835 - All drivers [*yezdovyye*] with the guns and caissons [*zaryadnye yashchiki*] are to have one **pistol** each, after the example of other lower ranks [200].

13 April 1835 - Officers in formation are to use a toggle [*kostylok*] to fasten one end of the **shako lines** [*kivernyi snur*] in back of the shako to an eye-loop [*petlya*] fashioned from the decorative cord [*etishketnyi snur*]. At all other times when officers are not in formation and must remove the shako, this line is unfastened from the eye-loop and, keeping it around the neck along with its slide [*gaika*], which is to be at the back at the middle of the neck, the end with the toggle is fastened to the second coat button from the top so that the line passes under the right arm and over the pouch-belt [201].

31 January 1836 - Lower ranks' **greatcoats** are to have eleven buttons instead of twelve: six down the front, two on the collar patches, two on the shoulder straps, and one behind on the flaps [202].

27 April 1836 - **Lower pompons** [*repeiki*] are to be lined with black leather [203].

9 October 1836 - To hold their **pistols**, trumpeters are to have holsters [*chushki*] attached to the saddle on the left side over the saddle cloth. For the cartridges they are to have pouches [*lyadunki*] with belts, like those of other lower ranks (Illus. 426) [204].

17 January 1837 - When wearing the **frock coat** without the sash, generals and field and company-grade officers are to wear the **saber** under the frock, attaching the upper ring to the hook next to the first sling and putting the hilt through an oblique pocket, in the same way as the half-saber and sword are worn in the Infantry. But when wearing the frock coat with the sash, the saber is to be over the coat, left free on its slings and not hung onto the hook [205].

14 February 1837 - Trumpeters, who are prescribed pistols when in mounted formation and cartridge-pouches with belts, are also to wear these **cartridge-pouches** when in dismounted formation [206].

15 July 1837 - The new pattern of officers' **sash** is approved, identical with that introduced at this time for regiments of Army Infantry and Cavalry and described above [207].

17 December 1837 - The new pattern of officers' **epaulettes** is approved, identical with that introduced at this time for Dragoon regiments, i.e. with the addition of a fourth twist of braid [208].

23 February 1838 - The regulations concerning the **pistol holsters** [*pistoletnyya chushki*] mandated for the saddle on 9 October 1836 are confirmed as laid out above for Dragoon regiments [209].

4 January 1839 - Officers' **riding-trousers** [*reituzy*] are not to have any bows or bands in front but rather worn completely plain in the manner prescribed for lower ranks [210].

16 October 1840 - Lower ranks who have earned the right to discharge on indefinite leave but who voluntarily remain on active service after completing the term of service are to be given gold galloon **chevrons** [*shevrony, ili nashivki*] to be sewn onto the left sleeve, one for every five years of extra service. On the same basis these same chevrons are to be given to non-commissioned officer fireworkers [*feierverkery*] who have declined promotion to officer rank and are receiving two-thirds of an ensign's pay for serving five or more years after declining such promotion [211].

23 January 1841 - The capes of officers' **greatcoats** are to be 28 inches long as measured from the lower edge of the collar [212].

13 November 1841 - All combatant ranks are given a new pattern of **saber** [*sablya*] identical with that introduced at this time for Dragoon regiments, but without a fitting for a bayonet (Illus. 427) [213].

8 April 1843 - The new model **shako** that curves inward at the bottom is approved, being identical to that confirmed at this time for Grenadier regiments (Illus. 428). In order to distinguish between the lower ranks, trimming [*nashivki*] on the **epaulettes** and **shoulder straps** is established on the same basis as described above for the Foot Artillery [214].

2 June 1843 - Approval is given to the same manner of positioning the **shako plate** as presented above for Grenadier regiments [215].

2 January 1844 - Officers are to have a **cockade** on the cap band of the forage cap, identical with that introduced at this time in the regiments of Army Infantry and Cavalry and described above (Illus. 429) [216].

9 May 1844 - Shakos are replaced by **helmets** with plumes, of the same pattern and in accordance with the same regulations as for Grenadier Artillery brigades at this time, but with the addition of a metal edging on the front peak, of the same color as the helmet mountings (Illus. 430 and 431) [217].

20 May 1844 - Approval is given to a new scheme for differentiating the **forage caps** of the lower ranks, according to which the piping around the top is to be red cloth while the cap band is black cloth with two red pipings, one on each edge, and with the battery number and letter cut out and backed by yellow cloth. Officers' cap bands are the same as for lower ranks but, as before, without numbers or letters [218].

4 January 1845 - Officers' **helmets** are to have, on the right side under the chin-scales, a cockade, as described above for Grenadier and other regiments of Army Infantry (Illus. 432) [219].

The special statute ***"Badges for distinction"*** [*"Znaki otlichii"*] gives a detailed list of Horse-Artillery batteries which for military feats have been awarded badges for distinction to be worn on the shako or gold lace bars [*petlitsy*] for officers' coats, in accordance with the usage accepted during previous reigns. By 1 January 1846 these badges and lace bars were as follows:

a.) Badges inscribed "*Za otlichie*" ["For excellence"] — Heavy Batteries №№15 and 23 and Light Batteries №№1, 5, 7, 9, 16, and 24.

b.) Badges inscribed "*Za Varshavu 25 i 26 Avgusta 1831 goda*" ["For Warsaw 25 and 26 August of the year 1831"] — Light Batteries №№2, 3, 4, and 22.

c.) Gold lace bars — Heavy Batteries №№15, 23, and 25 and Light Batteries №№1, 5, 16, 24, and 26.

4 February 1846 - **Pistols** are abolished for drivers [*yezdovye*] [220].

13 September 1846 - Officers' **pistols** are to be of the new pattern with percussion locks, for which new **holsters** [*kobury*] to fit these locks are approved [221].

19 May 1847 - With the new, general directive concerning the colors for **forage caps** within the War Department [*Voennoe vedomstvo*, i.e. the entire army — M.C.], clerks, medics [*feldshera*], and other lower ranks of the Horse Artillery with dark-green forage caps are to have cap bands and piping around the top part in the same colors as the cap bands and piping of combatant lower ranks. Barbers, hospital orderlies, and others with grey forage caps are to have piping on both edges of the cap band and around the top in the same color as the facing cloth [222].

9 January 1848 - On those days when they are obliged to remain in ceremonial dress after the mounting of the guard, field and company-grade officers are permitted for walking-out to wear the **frock coat** and **riding-trousers** with **helmet** and **plume** (Illus.433) [223].

19 January 1848 - With the introduction of officers' **pistols** with percussion locks, Highest Authority approves the firing-cap pouch [*kapsulnaya sumochka*] with the cartridge-pouch as presented above in detail for Army Cuirassier regiments [224].

25 April 1848 - All flaps and buttons are removed from **valises** [225].

31 May 1849 - Field and company-grade officers of Replacement [*Zapasnaya*] Horse-Artillery batteries are not to have any **numbers** on buttons or epaulettes; buttons are to have only crossed cannons [226].

24 December 1849 - The grip on the hilt of the **gold saber** awarded for bravery is to be gold instead of wrapped in black, lacquered leather [227].

30 March 1851 - **Cartridge-pouch belts** are to be 1-3/4 inches wide and have the previous firing-cap pouch [228].

13 August 1853 - Generals and field and company-grade officers in the campaign dress of **frock coat** without sash are to buckle the sword-belt on over the coat [229].

18 February 1854 - The regulation of 15 November 1853 concerning light-cavalry **horse furniture**, presented above in the section for Army Cuirassier regiments, is also extended to the Horse Artillery (Illus. 434) [230].

29 April 1854 - Generals and field and company-grade officers, in wartime, are to have campaign **greatcoats** of the same color and pattern as the greatcoats of lower ranks, in accordance with the guidelines explained above for Cuirassier regiments (Illus. 434) [231].

NOTES TO THE ILLUSTRATIONS
By Mark Conrad

419. Horse-artillery uniforms were in the same color scheme as foot artillery. In this figure the pants have two wide stripes with a thin stripe in between. The shabraque is dark green with a wide red stripe and a thin red edge. The officer's pouch belt was gold with a silver badge, pickers, and chain.

427. The greatcoat has a black collar piped red with a red tab. Shoulder straps are also red.

429. The inside lining of the frock coat is red.

431. Notice that the top lace on the collar is non-commissioned officers' rank lace and not musicians' tape.

432 and 434. The shabraque is dark green with three thin red stripes, with black between the two inner stripes.

15 - SAPPER AND PIONEER BATTALIONS (*SAPERNYE I PIONERNYE BATALIONY*).

11 and 26 February 1826 - In place of the double-breasted coats, officers and lower ranks of Sapper and Pioneer battalions are given **single-breasted** ones with nine flat buttons down the front, red cuff-flaps, and red piping down the front and from the center to the turnbacks. Officers' grey riding-trousers and pants with high boots, and the lower ranks' pants with gaiters [*kragi*], are replaced with long dark-green **pants** with red piping down the side seams. Underneath these pants and over the boots, lower ranks at all times, but company-grade officers only when in formation or on parade [*tolko v stroyu i parade*], are to wear black cloth **half-gaiters** [*polushtiblety*] buttoned with five or six small buttons (Illus. 435 and 436). Along with this change the horizontal belt for the **knapsack** is to be worn between the two lower buttons on the front of the coat. The greatcoat is to be carried on top of the knapsack, rolled into a tube inside a special oilskin case made of raven's-duck (Illus. 436). Generals, field-grade officers, and adjutants are to wear boots with the **spurs** driven in. The **Lithuania Pioneer Battalion** [*Litovskii Pionernyi batalion*] keeps its coats with plastrons (Illus. 437) [232].

10 May 1826 - Generals, field-grade officers, and those company-grade officers who are mounted when in formation, are during the summer to wear white linen **pants** without integral spats [*kozyrki*], of the same pattern as previously described for the dark-green ones (Illus. 438). In addition, suede pants of the same pattern may be worn instead of the linen ones [233].

15 September 1826 - Lower ranks who have completed the regulation number of years of faultless service but who voluntarily remain on active duty are to wear **gold galloon** sewn onto the left sleeve as related above for Grenadier regiments [234].

1 January 1827 - Officers are to have little gold forged and stamped stars as rank distinctions on their **epaulettes**, regardless of monograms or letters. These are of the same form and in the same scheme as for other troops of Army Infantry and Cavalry described above [235].

14 February 1827 - The **pocket flaps** of officers' coats are not to have red piping [236].

31 July 1827 - Numbers and letters on the **covers for shakos and cartridge-pouches**, instead of being of yellow cloth, are to be painted in yellow oil paint [237].

19 November 1827 - Highest Authority reaffirms that on coats and greatcoats, the lower edge of the **collar** is to have red cloth piping [238].

14 December 1827 - The **chevrons** established on 15 September 1826 for the left sleeve of lower ranks are to be silver and made from non-commissioned officers' galloon [239].

24 March 1828 - The **coats** of lower ranks are not to be tailored with cinches [240].

24 April 1828 - Officers and lower ranks of the Sapper and Pioneer battalions are given a new pattern **shako**, identical with that introduced at this time for regiments of Army Infantry, i.e. higher that before, without the leather straps stitched on the sides, and with a white cord around the top. Pompons for these shakos are as before: in the Sapper Battalion and the Sapper platoons of Pioneer battalions — red; in the Miner platoons of Pioneer battalions — yellow; in the Pioneer companies of Pioneer battalions — white. **Shako plates** are prescribed as for Army Infantry, but of white tin-plate with two crossed axes, above which there is to be a single-flamed grenade for the Sapper Battalion (Illus. 439 and 440) and a cut-out figure of the battalion number for Pioneer battalions (Illus. 441 and 442). Together with this the following changes are also introduced:

1.) The width of **crossbelts** and **swordbelts** is stipulated to be 3 1/2 inches; that of knapsack shoulder straps - 2 5/8 inches; and of the strap across the chest - 2 inches.

2.) **Knapsacks** are to be of calfskin as before but with black leather trim. The knapsack is prescribed to be 15 3/4 inches broad, 14 inches high, and 4 3/8 inches wide. From the upper edge the length of the cover is 10 1/2 inches.

3.) In general all non-combatant personnel of non-commissioned officer rank are given dark-green **frock coats** [*syurtuki*] with a single row of buttons to replace their grey coats [*mundiry*] now in use. The frock coats have the same collar, cuffs, and shoulder straps as for combatant personnel, but the pants are grey with red piping on the side seams.

4.) Non-combatant craftsmen of the lower ranks, as well as medical orderlies, are to replace their coats [*mundiry*] with grey cloth **jackets** [*kurtki*] modeled on the coat. Pants are to be as for the non-combatants above [241].

10 August 1828 - In place of shakos, the **Caucasus Pioneer Battalion** [*Kavkazskii Pionernyi batalion*] is given a **sheepskin headdress** [*shapka*] identical to that introduced at this time for the Infantry of the Separate Caucasus Corps (Illus. 443) [242].

16 December 1829 - The black cuffs of officers' **frock coats** are changed to dark green, with red piping as before [243].

26 December 1829 - Upon the renaming of Pioneer battalions to Sappers, and of the former Sapper Battalion to the Grenadier Sapper Battalion, all combatant lower ranks are to have uniform **buttons** with the raised image of two small, crossed axes, above which there is a representation of a single-flamed grenade for the Grenadier Sapper Battalion and the numbers and letters as on the shako plate for the other battalions (Illus. 444) [244].

14 March 1830 - The battalions renamed from Pioneers to Sappers keep their former uniform, without the lace bars which are prescribed only for the Grenadier Sapper Battalion. Together with this, **letters** and **numbers** on officers' epaulettes and lower ranks' shoulder straps are to be as follows: Grenadier Sapper Battalion — Cyrillic *G.S.*; 1st Sapper Battalion — Cyrillic *1.S.*; 2nd — Cyrillic *2.S.*; 3rd — Cyrillic *3.S.*; 4th — Cyrillic *4.S.*; 5th — Cyrillic *5.S.*; 1st Reserve Sapper Battalion — Cyrillic *1.R.S.*; 2nd Reserve — Cyrillic *2.R.S.*; 3rd Reserve — Cyrillic *3.R.S.*; Lithuania Sapper Battalion — Cyrillic *L.S.*; Caucasus Sapper Battalion — Cyrillic *K.S.* The device on the shield on the shako plate is to be: Grenadier Sapper Battalion — two axes and a grenade; 1st, 2nd, 3rd, 4th, and 5th Sapper Battalions — two axes and the battalion number; 1st, 2nd, and 3rd Reserve Sapper Battalions — the battalion number and the Cyrillic letter *R.*; Lithuania Sapper Battalion — the Cyrillic letter *L.*; Caucasus Sapper Battalion — the Cyrillic letter *L.* All these letters and numbers are cut out. Together with this the upper **pompons** of lower ranks in the Sapper battalions and the lower pompons of all privates [*ryadovye*] are to be red. Also, in all battalions there is a triple-flamed grenade on the cartridge-pouch [*suma*], regardless of the company [245].

6 April 1830 - The **3rd Reserve Sapper Battalion** (2nd Reserve Sapper Battalion from 23 December 1841) is awarded a white tin-plate badge for the shako with the cut-out inscription "*Za otlichie*" ["For excellence"] [246].

20 August 1830 - The officers' former **rapiers** [*shpagi*] are replaced by half-sabers [*polusabli*] like those approved at this time for Grenadier and other regiments of the Army Infantry (Illus. 445) [247].

22 September 1830 - The **Caucasus Sapper Battalion** is awarded a white tin-plate badge for the shapka headdress with the inscription "*Za otlichie*" (Illus. 445) [248].

9 May 1831 - The **6th Sapper Battalion**, renamed from the Lithuania Sapper Battalion, is prescribed the same uniform as the 1st, 2nd, 3rd, 4th, and 5th Sapper Battalions, i.e. without plastrons, and with the number 6 on epaulettes, shoulder straps, buttons, and shako plates [249].

8 June 1832 - Officers are permitted to wear **moustaches** [250].

3 January 1833 - Cloth **half-gaiters** [*polustiblety*] are abolished for company-grade officers and lower ranks. **Covers** for shakos and cartridge-pouches, along with **sword knots**, are abolished for non-commissioned officers and privates (Illus. 446). These sword knots are only to be retained by those non-commissioned officers who have them in silver [251].

20 January 1833 - **Covers** for the shako are restored as before [252].

20 February 1833 - All combatant personnel are given a new pattern of summer **pants** or **trousers** [*pantalony ili bryuki*] without buttons or integral spats (Illus. 447) [253].

22 February 1833 - Field and company-grade officers are not to use the hat, but rather wear the **shako** at all times. Officers who must be mounted when in formation are permitted to have **horses** with long tails [254].

5 May 1833 - The characters or numbers and letters on **shako plates** are not to be cut out, but rather are to be fixed on, in brass for lower ranks and gilded for officers (Illus. 448 and 449) [255].

28 March 1834 - Highest Authority confirms the new pattern of **short-sword** [*tesak*] with yellow brass mountings and a straight blade, identical to that introduced at this time in the Army Foot Artillery [256].

26 September 1834 - Lower ranks are directed to wear the **knapsack** on two belts lying crosswise over the chest (Illus. 450) [257].

20 August 1835 - Officers are directed to wear the **knapsack** using only two shoulder belts; there are to be no straps that cross over the front of the body or the chest. These belts are to be lacquered. For lower ranks a linen case or pocket for the forage cap is to be put on the outside of the knapsack on the side that lies on the soldier's back. These cases are to be made from the linings of worn-out coats. For drummers the knapsack is worn over the shoulder on one belt as before [258].

31 January 1836 - The lower ranks' **greatcoat** is to have nine buttons instead of ten: six down the front, two on the shoulder straps, and one on the flaps behind [259].

27 April 1836 - **Lower pompons** [*repeiki*] are to be lined with black leather [260].

13 May 1836 - Girths for officers' **saddles** are to be dark green with red stripes [261].

14 January 1837 - Handles of **entrenching tools** are to have the wooden parts varnished, and the same directives for the fitting and carrying of these tools apply as described above in detail for Grenadier regiments [262].

15 June 1837 - Approval is given to the new pattern of officers' **sash**, identical with that introduced at this time in regiments of Army infantry and cavalry and described above [263].

17 December 1837 - Approval is given to a new pattern of officers' **epaulettes** identical to those introduced at this time in regiments of Army infantry and cavalry, i.e. with the addition of a fourth twist of braid [264].

4 January 1839 - Generals and field and company-grade officers are not to have any bows or bands on the front of their **pants** or **trousers**. These are to be worn completely plain in the manner prescribed for lower ranks [265].

16 March 1839 - Lower ranks' **pouch-belts** and **swordbelts** are to be 2 3/5 inches wide, while drummers' **crossbelts** are 4 2/5 inches wide as before [266].

16 October 1840 - The regulation is confirmed concerning **silver galloon** or **chevrons** for lower ranks, as laid out above for Grenadier regiments [267].

23 January 1841 - The capes of officers' **greatcoats** are to be 28 inches long as measured from the lower edge of the collar [268].

26 November 1842 - Until the approval of a new uniform, the Caucasus Sapper Battalion is to wear the **forage cap** instead of the sheepskin shapka headdress [269].

8 April 1843 - A new pattern **shako** curving inward at the bottom is approved, identical to that confirmed at this time for Grenadier and other regiments of Army infantry as well as for cavalry and artillery (Illus. 451). Also approved is the trimming on the **shoulder straps** of sergeants [*feldfebeli*], non-commissioned officers [*unter-ofitsery*], and lance-corporals [*yefreitory*], following the same scheme as for Grenadier regiments. For Grenadier Sappers the trimming has a red stripe while for others it is all white. At this same time, in order to be more easily distinguished from field-grade officers' epaulettes, it is directed that **drum-majors' epaulettes** have red silk between the braided gold threads and in the hanging fringe (Illus. 452). Along with all this, the cut-out letters on the **shoulder straps** of the Grenadier Sapper Battalion are to be cursive [*kursivnyi*] [270].

2 June 1843 - The method of fitting the shako plate and badge for distinction to the **shako** is confirmed, according to which the lower edge of the shako plate, with or without the badge for distinction, is to lie at the point halfway across the width of the lacquered shako binding, with the cross on the crown in the plate lying on the lower edge of the badge for distinction. The badge for distinction itself is to be even with the top of the shako [271].

2 January 1844 - Officers are to have a **cockade** on the band of the forage cap, identical to that introduced at this time in the regiments of Army infantry and cavalry and described above [272].

9 May 1844 - The shako is replaced by a **helmet** of the same pattern as established at this time for regiments of Army infantry. In the Grenadier Sapper Battalion the helmet has a black, horsehair plume while other battalions have no plume (Illus. 453 and 454). The Caucasus Sapper Battalion keeps the **forage cap** [273].

20 May 1844 - With the approval of a new general listing for distinctive **forage caps**, a Sapper battalion keeps its previous dark-green ones with red cloth piping around the top and on both edges of the cap band and cutout letters (for lower ranks) backed by yellow cloth. In the first Sapper companies [*roty*] these are Cyrillic *1.S.R.*, in the first Miner companies — Cyrillic *1.M.R.*, in the first Pioneer companies — Cyrillic *1.P.R.*, etc. Cap bands are the same for officers as for lower ranks but, as before, without numbers or letters [274].

4 January 1845 - Officers' **helmets** are to have a cockade on the right side under the chin-scales, as related above for Grenadier and other regiments of Army infantry (Illus. 455) [275].

9 August 1845 - In the Grenadier Sapper Battalion, in camp dress [*lagernaya forma*] **helmets** are to be worn without plumes, even if personnel entitled to them are wearing coats [*mundiry*] [276].

23 June 1846 - With the introduction of weapons with percussion gun-locks, approval is given to the description for fitting the **firing-cap pouch** as laid out in detail above for Grenadier regiments (Illus. 456) [277].

6 January 1848 - On those days when they are obliged to remain in ceremonial dress after the mounting of the guard, field and company-grade officers are permitted for walking-out to wear the **frock coat** with **helmet** and **plume** [277].

8 August 1848 - The **Caucasus and 3rd Reserve Sapper Battalions** are prescribed the new uniform and equipment confirmed at this time and described above in detail for Grenadier regiments (Illus. 457 and 458) [278].

19 April 1849 - With the introduction of new English **signal bugles**, approval is given to the method of fitting a belt to them as described above in detail for Grenadier regiments (Illus. 459) [279].

28 April 1849 - Approval is given to the following description of fitting the **greatcoat** above the **ammunition pouch** [*patrontash*] in the Caucasus and 3rd Reserve Sapper Battalions:

The greatcoat, tightly rolled into a round tube, 15 3/4 inches long, is held above the ammunition pouch by the cloak-belt [*plashchevoi remen*]. The pointed end of this belt passes down under the waistbelt [*poyasnoi remen*] and then from below through a loop stitched to the center of the ammunition pouch. It then goes over the greatcoat and fastens to a buckle so that the loop is right on the waist. After the pointed end passes through the loop at the buckle, it again goes under the waistbelt to be let down underneath the ammunition pouch [280].

14 September 1849 - Confirmation is made as to the pattern of **percussion pistol** for officers, as related above for Grenadier regiments [281].

9 and 25 November 1849 - Approval is given to the fitting of the **helmet** as described above in detail for Grenadier reg. [282].

24 December 1849 - The grip of the hilt of the **gold half-saber** awarded for bravery is to be gold instead of being wrapped with black, lacquered leather [283].

17 January 1851 - Approval is given to the descriptions laid out above for Grenadier regiments for folding up and turning back the skirts of the **greatcoat** (Illus. 460) [284].

21 March 1851 - In the Caucasus and 3rd Reserve Sapper Battalions the **ammunition pouch** is to have places for 40 rounds instead of 60 [285].

8 July 1851 - The **gun-lock covers** [*polunagalishcha*] are abolished and approval given to the patterns and descriptions of the **drum**, **fife case** for Caucasus troops, **water flask**, **greatcoat strap**, **swordbelt**, **crossbelt**, and **cover for the firing nipple** of percussion weapons, all as presented above for Grenadier regiments [286].

20 October 1851 - The list and description of items to be carried by the soldier in his **knapsack** while on the march and during inspections is confirmed as laid out above for Grenadier regiments [287].

26 January 1852 - Non-combatant lower ranks with grey cloth **forage caps** are to have cloth cap bands of the same color as the collar [of combatant personnel — M.C.] [288].

3 January 1853 - Non-combatant lower ranks with **frock coats** are to have these reach to the lower part of the knee [289].

18 February 1854 - Field-grade officers and battalion adjutants are to have a valise and greatcoat on their **saddle** according to the directives presented above for Grenadier regiments [290].

29 April 1854 - Field and company-grade officers in wartime are to have campaign **greatcoats**, and company-grade officers are to wear the swordbelt over the shoulder. Both of these directives are to be carried out just as established for Grenadier regiments at this time and according to the same guidelines [291].

13 February 1855 - The new manner of fitting the **firing-cap pouch** is confirmed as presented above for Grenadier regiments [292].

NOTES TO THE ILLUSTRATIONS
By Mark Conrad

435. Engineers had the same uniform colors as the artillery but with silver metal buttons and appointments and solid red turnbacks.

438. The shabraque is dark green with two silver lace stripes.

441. The greatcoat has red shoulder straps with the yellow number 1 and Cyrillic letter P for Pioneer, along with a black collar piped red.

454. The seated figure has red shoulder straps with the yellow Cyrillic letters GS for Grenadier Sapper Battalion. The drummer's plume is red.

457 and 458. For the new uniforms of the Caucasus Corps, collars, shoulder straps, and piping were as for the previous tailed coats. The piped cuffs, though, were dark green.

459. The base color of the swallow's-nests appears to be red.

460. The greatcoat has a black collar piped red and red shoulder straps with yellow letters.

Emperor Nicholas I annouces to his guard outbreak of November Uprising in Poland

16 - HORSE PIONEERS (*KONNYE PIONERY*).

11 February 1826 - Clerks and in general all non-combatant lower ranks are to have grey **riding-trousers** with red stripes [293].

26 February 1826 - For the 1st Horse-Pioneer Squadron [*1-i Konno-Pionernyi eskadron*] the **coat** [*mundir*] is to have cuffs with red cloth cuff-flaps as in the infantry (Illus. 461) [294].

12 July 1826 - The squadron's former dark-green pants with red stripes and grey riding-trousers likewise with stripes are replaced by **riding-trousers** of grey cloth, without stripes, but with black cloth piping on the side seams (Illus. 461) [295].

15 September 1826 - Lower ranks who have completed the regulation number of years of faultless service and have the right to be discharged but voluntarily remain on active duty are to wear **gold galloon** sewn onto the left sleeve above and in addition to the yellow tape [*bason*] prescribed on 26 March 1825 [296].

1 January 1827 - Officers' **epaulettes** are to have small gold forged and stamped stars as rank distinctions, without regard to monograms, of the same pattern and scheme as for the other troops of Army infantry and cavalry described earlier [297].

31 July 1827 - Numbers and letters on the **covers** for shakos are changed from yellow cloth to being painted with yellow oil paint [298].

8 October 1827 - A new pattern of **saber** is approved, straighter and with a brass hilt, black grip, and iron scabbard (Illus. 462) [299].

13 October 1827 - All combatant ranks are given **scaled epaulettes** for the coat in the same color as the buttons, with a backing and strap of red cloth and a brass (gold for officers) figure *1*. (Illus. 462) [300].

14 December 1827 - The lower ranks' **chevrons** established for the left sleeve on 15 September are to be silver and made from non-commissioned officers' galloon [301].

12 January 1828- Instead of black, the piping on **riding-trousers** is to be of red cloth (Illus. 463) [302].

9 February 1828 - A new model of **shako** is issued, identical with that established at this time for all the cavalry, with upper and lower pompons [*pompon i repeika*] and a decorative cord, all in yellow (silver for officers). The metal mountings on the shako remain the same as before (Illus. 463) [303].

24 April 1828 - In general all non-combatant personnel of non-commissioned officer rank are given dark-green **frock coats** with a single row of buttons to replace their grey coats now in use. These frock coats have the same collar, cuffs, and shoulder straps as for combatant personnel, but the pants are grey with red piping on the side seams. Non-combatant lower-rank craftsmen, as well as medical orderlies, are to replace the coats now in use with grey cloth **jackets** modeled on the coat, while pants are to be as for the non-combatants above [304].

20 December 1828 - The squadron's **shakos**, in place of the previous plate with star, crown, and device depicting two axes, are to have the same plate as prescribed on 24 April for the 1st Pioneer Battalion, i.e. with a device consisting of two axes within a shield and the cut-out number and the Cyrillic letters *1.K.P.* (Illus. 464) [305].

16 December 1829 - The black cuffs of officers' **frock coats** are changed to dark green, with red piping as before [306].

26 December 1829 - All combatant personnel are to have uniform **buttons** with a raised representation of two small crossed axes, above which are the number and the Cyrillic letters *1.K.P.* [307].

3 January 1833 - **Shako covers** are abolished [308].

20 January 1833 - **Shako covers** are restored as before [309].

22 February 1833 - Field and company-grade officers are not to use the hat, but rather use the **shako** at all times [310].

16 March 1833 - The **undress coat** [*vitse-mundir*] of field and company-grade officers is abolished [311].

5 May 1833 - The numbers and letters on **shako plates** are not to be cut out, but rather are to be fixed on, in yellow brass for lower ranks (Illus. 465) and gilded for officers [312].

13 April 1834 - **Pouches** and **pouch-belts** are to be of the new pattern with a smaller cover and narrower belt [313].

2 May 1834 - For better handling, the hilts of the **sabers** are to be reworked in the new style as explained above for Dragoon regiments [314].

7 December 1834 - When shakos are worn, the **shako lines** [*snury u kiverov*] are not to reach to the waist, but only halfway down the back [315].

4 January 1835 - Privates are to begin using **gloves** [*perchatki*] of greyish-blue cloth, made from worn-out riding-trousers. These are only to be worn at times when infantry troops would be wearing their own cloth mittens [*rukavitsy*]. Non-commissioned officers keep their deerskin gloves [*losinnyya perchatki*] as before [316].

13 April 1835 - Officers in formation are to use a toggle [*kostylok*] to fasten one end of the **shako lines** [*kivernyi snur*] in back of the shako to an eye-loop [*petlya*] fashioned from the decorative cord [*etishketnyi snur*]. At all other times when officers are not in formation and must remove the shako, this line is unfastened from the eye-loop and, keeping it around the neck along with its slide [*gaika*], which is to be at the back at the middle of the neck, the end with the toggle is fastened to the second coat button from the top so that the line passes under the right arm and over the pouch-belt [317].

31 January 1836 - Lower ranks' **greatcoats** are to have eleven buttons instead of twelve: six down the front, two on the collar patches, two on the shoulder straps, and one behind on the flaps [318].

27 April 1836 - **Lower pompons** [*repeiki*] are to be lined with black leather [319].

9 October 1836 - In order to carry their **pistols**, trumpeters are to have holsters [*chushki*] attached to the saddle on the left side over the saddle cloth. For the cartridges they are to have pouches [*lyadunki*] with belts, like those of other lower ranks [320].

17 January 1837 - When wearing the **frock coat** without the sash, generals and field and company-grade officers are to wear the **saber** under the frock, attaching the upper ring to the hook next to the first sling and putting the hilt through an oblique pocket, in the same way as the half-saber and sword are worn in the infantry. But when wearing the frock coat with the sash, the saber is to be over the coat, left free on its slings and not hung onto the hook [321].

14 February 1837 - Trumpeters, who are prescribed pistols when in mounted formation and likewise pouches with belts for their cartridges, are also to wear these **cartridge-pouches** when in dismounted formation [322].

15 July 1837 - The new pattern of officers' **sash** is approved, identical with that introduced at this time for regiments of Army Infantry and Cavalry and described above [323].

17 December 1837 - The new pattern of officers' **epaulettes** is approved, identical with that introduced at this time for Dragoon regiments, i.e. with the addition of a fourth twist of braid [324].

23 February 1838 - The regulations concerning the **pistol holsters** [*pistoletnyya chushki*] mandated for the saddle on 9 October 1836 are confirmed as laid out above for Dragoon regiments [325].

4 January 1839 - Officers' **riding-trousers** [*reituzy*] are not to have any bows or bands in front but rather worn completely plain in the manner prescribed for lower ranks [326].

16 October 1840 - The regulation concerning silver **chevrons** for lower ranks is confirmed as laid out above for Grenadier regiments [327].

23 January 1841 - The capes of officers' **greatcoats** are to be 28 inches long as measured from the lower edge of the collar [328].

13 November 1841 - All combatant ranks are given a new pattern of **saber** identical with that introduced at this time for Dragoon regiments, but without a fitting for a bayonet (Illus. 466) [329].

8 April 1843 - The new model **shako** that curves inward at the bottom is approved, being identical to that confirmed at this time for Grenadier regiments (Illus. 467). Sewn-on trim [*nashivki*] is established for the shoulder straps of sergeants [*vakhtmistry*, from German *Wachtmeister* — M.C.], non-commissioned officers [*unter-ofitsery*], and lance corporals [*yefreitory*], based on the same scheme as described above for Dragoon regiments [330].

10 May 1843 - Covers for the **cartridge-pouch** are to measure (when attached to the body of the pouch) 7 7/8 inches long, 8 1/2 inches wide at the top edge, and 9 7/8 inches wide at the bottom edge [331].

2 June 1843 - Approval is given to the same manner of positioning the **shako plate** as is presented above for Grenadier regiments [332].

2 January 1844 - Officers are to have a **cockade** on the cap band of the forage cap, identical with that introduced at this time in the regiments of Army infantry and cavalry and described above [333].

9 May 1844 - Shakos are replaced by **helmets** with plumes, of the same pattern and in accordance with the same regulations as for the Grenadier Sapper Battalion at this time, but with the addition of a metal edging on the front peak, of the same color as the helmet mountings (Illus. 468 and 469) [334].

20 May 1844 - Based on the new general scheme for **forage caps**, they remain dark green in the 1st Horse Pioneer Squadron, with red cloth piping around the top and both edges of the cap band and (for lower ranks) the cut-out number and the Cyrllic letters *1.K.P.* backed by yellow cloth. Officers' cap bands are the same as for lower ranks but, as before, without numbers or letters [335].

4 January 1845 - Officers' **helmets** are to have, on the right side under the chin-scales, a cockade, as described above for Grenadier and other regiments of Army infantry (Illus. 470) [336].

9 August 1845 - In camp dress [*lagernaya forma*], helmets are to be worn without plumes, even if personnel entitled to them are wearing their coats [*mundiry*] [337].

31 March 1846 - The 1st Horse-Pioneer Battalion [*1-i Konno-Pionernyi divizion*] is to have new-model artillery sabers and dragoon muskets, the manner and fitting of which is to be the same as for dragoons (Illus. 471) [338].

7 August 1846 - Approval is given to the following description of fitting firing-cap pouches and tin cases, and to the manner of stowing both these items as well as the small valise and the percussion-cap turnscrew:

1.) The **firing-cap pouch** [*kapsyulnaya sumochka*] is to be lined inside with fur with the nap down so that the caps cannot fall out during violent movements. These pouches are fitted on the right side of the chest and button underneath the cartridge-pouch crossbelt so that the lower edge of the pouch is even with the fourth coat button from the bottom. These pouches are buttoned to the crossbelt with two buttons by means of a strap of stiff leather with must be wider than in the infantry. The pouch cover is closed using the same strap, the end of which is to be folded under so that it does not hang down.

2.) **Tin cases** [*Zhestyanye futlyary*] for keeping spare firing caps are to be stored in the right side of the valise.

3.) **Small valises** [*Chemodanchiki*] with the soldier's sundries are to be made of cloth of the same color as the uniform and stored in the left holster [*kobura*].

4.) **Percussion-cap turnscrews** [*Pistonnyya otvertki*] are to be stored under the cover of the cartridge-pouch [339].

13 September 1846 - Officers' **pistols** are to be of the new pattern with percussion locks, for which new **holsters** [*kobury*] to fit these locks are approved, as related above in detail for Cuirassier regiments [340].

5 November 1847 - In those circumstances when lower ranks in mounted formation are to use the greatcoat as a cloak [*shineli v nakidku*], they are to wear these over the accouterments and using the sleeves, with the front open. In dismounted formation, however, the wearing of the greatcoat is to be as before [341].

17 November 1847 - The 1st Horse-Pioneer Battalion is to have leather cases for their muskets [*kozhanye chekhly pri ruzhikh*], with straps and buckles, after the example of the Horse Grenadier and Dragoon regiments of the Life-Guards [342].

9 January 1848 - On those days when they are obliged to remain in ceremonial dress after the mounting of the guard, field and company-grade officers of the 1st Horse-Pioneer Battalion are permitted for walking-out to wear the **frock coat** and **riding-trousers** with **helmet** and **plume** [343].

19 January 1848 - With the introduction of officers' **pistols** with percussion locks, Highest Authority approves the firing-cap pouch [*kapsulnaya sumochka*] with the cartridge-pouch as presented above in detail for Army Cuirassier regiments [344].

25 April 1848 - All flaps and buttons are removed from **valises** [345].

5 March 1850 - The **bandolier** [*pantaler*] for the standard is to be 4 3/8 inches wide and 56 inches long, lined with cloth (black on the outside and dark green on the inside), with the fringe, galloon, and hook with bracket all silver [346].

30 March 1851 - **Cartridge-pouch belts** are to be 1 3/4 inches wide and have the previous firing-cap pouch [347].

15 April 1851 - Approval is given to the instructions for fitting straps to the valise for lower ranks in dismounted order [*dlya peshikh nizhnikh chinov*], which were also directed to personnel on leave from the cavalry [*dlya lyudei, uvolnyaemykh v otpuski iz kavaleriiskikh voisk*] and presented above in detail for Cuirassier regiments [348].

13 August 1853 - Generals and field and company-grade officers in the campaign dress of **frock coat** without sash are to buckle the sword-belt on over the coat [349].

18 February 1854 - The regulation of 15 November 1853 concerning light-cavalry **horse furniture**, presented above in the section for Army Cuirassier regiments, is also extended to Horse Pioneers [350].

29 April 1854 - Generals and field and company-grade officers, in wartime, are to have campaign **greatcoats** of the same color and pattern as the greatcoats of lower ranks [351].

NOTES TO THE ILLUSTRATIONS
By Mark Conrad

461. Like other engineer troops, horse pioneers had dark-green uniforms with black collars and cuffs piped red, red shoulder straps and cuff flaps, solid red turnbacks, and silver metal buttons and appointments. Around 1820 the shako pompon was yellow.

464. The shabraque is dark green with a wide red band, a thin red edge, and a red crowned Cyrillic N. The axhead is in a black case with a black strap around the end of the handle.

468. Being mounted troops, the horse pioneers have helmets with a metal edge on the front peak,

471. The blade of the shovel is in a black case.

NOTES

(1) Collection of Laws and Directives, 1826, Book II, pg. 183.
(2) Ibid., Book III, pg. 255.
(3) Ibid., Book IV, pg. 103.
(4) Ibid., 1827, Book I, pg. 3.
(5) Information received from the Commissariat Department of the War Ministry.
(6) Ibid.
(7) Collection of Laws and Directives, 1827, Book II, pg. 279.
(8) Ibid., Book IV, pg. 257.
(9) Ibid., 1828, Book I, pg. 211.
(10) Collection of Laws and Directives, 1829, Book IV, pg. 115, and information from the Commissariat Department of the War Ministry.
(11) Ibid., 1832, Book II, pg. 545.
(12) Information from the Commissariat Department of the War Ministry.
(13) Collection of Laws and Directives, 1834, Book II, pg. 237.
(14) Ibid., pgs. 245-247.
(15) Ibid., 1835, Book I, pg. 365.
(16) Ibid., pg. 319.
(17) Ibid., pg. 245.
(18) Ibid., Book III, pg. 145.
(19) Ibid., 1836, Book I, pg. 137.
(20) Ibid., Book III, pg. 115, § 7.
(21) Ibid., Book IV, pg. 153.
(22) Ibid., 1837, Book I, pg. 133.
(23) Ibid., Book III , pg. 47.
(24) Ibid., pg. 103.
(25) Ibid., Book IV, pg. 325.
(26) Ibid., 1839, Book I, pg. 3.
(27) Order of the Minister of War, 21 [sic, should be 16 - M.C.] October 1840, №71.
(28) Ibid., 23 January 1841, №8.
(29) Ibid., 8 April 1843, №44, §§ 6-11, and №46.
(30) Order of the Minister of War, 2 January 1844, №1.
(31) Ibid., 20 May 1844, №69, pgs. 8 and 9.
(32) Ibid., 21 September 1844, №115.
(33) Ibid., 27 January 1845, №17.
(34) Ibid., 5 February 1845, №21.
(35) Highest Directive to the Commissariat Department of the War Ministry, 7 September 1847, №9,017.
(36) Order of the Minister of War, 9 January 1848, №8.
(37) Ibid., 25 April 1848, №80.
(38) Ibid., 24 December 1849, №133.
(39) Ibid., 30 March 1851, №36.
(40) Ibid., 24 January 1853, №6.
(41) Ibid., 31 January 1853, №8.
(42) Ibid., 13 August 1853, №61.
(43) Ibid., 18 February 1854, №21.
(44) Ibid., 29 April 1854, №53.
(45) Collection of Laws and Directives, 1826, Book III, pg. 255.
(46) Ibid., 1827, Book I, pg. 3.
(47) Ibid., Book IV, pgs. 17-19, and papers from the Commissariat Department of the War Ministry.
(48) Collection of Laws and Directives, 1827, Book IV, pg. 257.
(49) Ibid., 1828, Book I, pg. 211.
(50) Ibid., 1829, Book I, pg. 241.
(51) Ibid., Book IV, pg. 19.
(52) Ibid., pg. 118.
(53) Ibid., 1830, Book I, pg. 13.
(54) Ibid., Book III, pg. 233.
(55) Complete Collection of Laws of the Russian Empire, 2nd Collection, Vol. VI, pg. 2, № 4,861, § 7.

(56) Collection of Laws and Directives, 1833, Book I, pg. 419.
(57) Ibid., Book IV, pg. 35.
(58) Ibid., Book I, pg. 22.
(59) Ibid., pg. 465.
(60) Ibid., pg. 242.
(61) Papers from the Commissariat Department of the War Ministry.
(62) Collection of Laws and Directives, 1833, Book IV, pg. 156.
(63) Papers from the Commissariat Department of the War Ministry.
(64) Collection of Laws and Directives, 1834, Book II, pg. 245.
(65) Ibid., pg. 249.
(66) Ibid., 1836, Book I, pg. 137.
(67) Ibid., Book II, pg. 171.
(68) Ibid., 1837, Book I, pg. 133.
(69) Ibid., Book III, pg. 47.
(70) Ibid., Book IV, pg. 325.
(71) Ibid., 1839, Book I, pg. 3.
(72) Ibid., Book III, pg. 41.
(73) Ibid., pg. 115.
(74) Order of the Minister of War, 16 October 1840, №71.
(75) Ibid., 29 October 1840, №75.
(76) Ibid., 23 January 1841, №8.
(77) Ibid., 6 June 1841, №50.
(78) Archives of the Commissariat Department of the War Ministry, papers from 1842, Section 2, 2nd Office, №365.
(79) Orders of the Minister of War, 8 April 1843, №№44 (§ 11), 46, and 47.
(80) Ibid., 2 June 1843, №78.
(81) Instruction of the Minister of War to the Commissariat Department of the War Ministry, 29 November 1843, №15,702.
(82) Order of the Minister of War, 2 January 1844, №1.
(83) Ibid., 9 May 1844, №63.
(84) Ibid., 20 May 1844, №69, pgs. 20 and 21.
(85) Ibid., 23 September 1844, №116.
(86) Ibid., 4 January 1845, №1.
(87) Ibid., 19 May 1847, №86.
(88) Ibid., 25 April 1848, №80.
(89) Order of the War Ministry Director, 8 August, 23 September, 31 October, and 24 November 1848, №№148, 163, 184, and 197, and 25 November 1849, №118.
(90) Order of the Minister of War, 17 April 1852, №43.
(91) Ibid., 13 August 1853, №61.
(92) Ibid., 18 February 1854, №21.
(93) Ibid., 29 April 1854, №53.
(94) Collection of Laws and Directives, 1826, Book I, pgs. 105 and 125.
(95) Ibid., 1827, Book II, pg. 47.
(96) Ibid., Book II, pg. 255.
(97) Ibid., 1827, Book I, pg. 3.
(98) Ibid., pg. 153.
(99) Ibid., pg. 249.
(100) Ibid., Book III, pg. 89.
(101) Ibid., Book IV, pg. 267.
(102) Ibid., 1828, Book I, pg. 211.
(103) Ibid., Book II, pgs. 131 et seq.
(104) Ibid., Book III, pg. 81.
(105) Ibid., Book IV, pg. 57.
(106) Ibid., 1829, Book II, pg. 221, § 12.
(107) Ibid., Book III, pg. 129, and information received from the Commissariat Department of the War Ministry.
(108) Collection of Laws and Directives, 1829, Book IV, pg. 19.
(109) Ibid., pg. 107.
(110) Ibid., pg. 115.
(111) Ibid., 1830, Book III, pg. 179.
(112) Ibid., 1831, Book I, pg. 71.

(113) Ibid., pg. 39.

(114) Order of the Director of the His Imperial Majesty's Main Staff, 1 January 1832, № 1.

(115) Ibid., 1832, Book II, pg. 545.

(116) Ibid., 1833, Book I, pg. 419.

(117) Ibid., pg. 435.

(118) Ibid., pg. 463.

(119) Ibid., pg. 465.

(120) Papers from the Commissariat Department of the War Ministry.

(121) Information received from the Artillery Department of the War Ministry, and a model sword confirmed by HIGHEST AUTHORITY.

(122) Collection of Laws and Directives, 1834, Book II, pg. 243.

(123) Ibid., pg. 257.

(124) Ibid., pg. 163.

(125) Ibid., Book III, pg. 429.

(126) Ibid., pg. 465.

(127) Ibid., 1835, Book III, pg. 179.

(128) Ibid., 1836, Book I, pg. 137.

(129) Information received from the Commissariat Department of the War Ministry.

(130) Ibid., 1836, Book II, pg. 171.

(131) Ibid., Book IV, pg. 157.

(132) Ibid., 1837, Book I, pg. 353.

(133) Ibid., Book III, pg. 47.

(134) Ibid., Book IV, pg. 325.

(135) Ibid., 1839, Book I, pg. 3.

(136) Ibid., pg. 179.

(137) Order of the Minister of War, 16 October 1840, №60.

(138) Ibid., 23 January 1841, №8.

(139) Archives of the Commissariat Department of the War Ministry, papers from 1842, Section 2, 2nd Office, № 365.

(140) Orders of the Minister of War, 8 April 1843, №№44 and 46.

(141) Order of the Minister of War, 2 June 1843, №78.

(142) Note from an instruction of the Minister of War to the Commissariat Department, 29 November 1843, №15,702.

(143) Order of the Minister of War, 2 January 1844, №1.

(144) Ibid., 9 May 1844, №№63 and 64.

(145) Ibid., 20 May 1844, N 69.

(146) Ibid., 4 January 1845, № 1.

(147) Description of lower ranks' forage caps, appended to the Order of the Minister of War, 19 May 1847, № 86.

(148) Order of the Minister of War., 9 January 1848, № 8.

(149) Order of the War Ministry Director, 8 August, 23 September, 31 October, and 24 November 1848, №№ 148, 163, 184, and 197, and 25 November 1849, № 118.

(150) Order of the Minister of War., 16 September 1848, № 162.

(151) Ibid., 31 October 1848, № 184.

(152) Ibid., 24 November 1848, № 197.

(153) Ibid., 14 September 1849, № 88.

(154) Ibid., 9 November 1849, № 110.

(155) Ibid., 25 November 1849, № 118.

(156) Ibid., 24 December 1849, № 133.

(157) Ibid., 28 May 1850, № 39.

(158) Ibid., 17 January 1851, № 7.

(159) Ibid., 13 December 1851, № 134.

(160) Ibid., 20 October 1851, № 120.

(161) Ibid., 26 January 1852, № 15.

(162) Ibid., 3 January 1853, № 3.

(163) Ibid., 18 February 1854, № 21.

(164) Ibid., 29 April 1854, № 53.

(165) Ibid., 16 June 1854, № 65.

(166) Ibid., 30 October 1854, № 119.

(167) Ibid., 19 January 1855, № 10.

(168) Collection of Laws and Directives, 1826, Book I, pg. 105.

(169) Ibid., pg. 125.

(170) Ibid., Book III, pg. 255.

(171) Ibid., Book IV, pg. 111.

(172) Ibid., 1827, Book I, pg. 3.

(173) Ibid., pg. 245.

(174) Ibid., Book III, pg. 89.

(175) Information received from the Commissariat Dep. of the War Ministry.

(176) Ibid.

(177) Collection of Laws and Directives, Book IV, pgs. 17 and 19.

(178) Ibid., pg. 267.

(179) Ibid., 1828, Book I, pg. 131.

(180) Ibid., Book IV, pg. 47.

(181) Ibid., 1829, Book IV, pg. 107.

(182) Ibid., pg. 115.

(183) Ibid., 1830, Book IV, pg. 401.

(184) Ibid., 1831, Book II, pg. 39.

(185) Ibid., Book IV, pg. 141.

(186) Ibid., 1833, Book I, pg. 419.

(187) Ibid., pg. 435.

(188) Ibid., pg. 465.

(189) Ibid., pg. 485.

(190) Papers from the Commissariat Department of the War Ministry.

(191) Ibid.

(192) Collection of Laws and Directives, 1834, Book II, pg. 243.

(193) Ibid., pgs. 245-247.

(194) Ibid., Book III, pg. 433.

(195) Ibid., pg. 429.

(196) Ibid., 1834, Book IV pg. 141.

(197) Ibid., pg. 257.

(198) Ibid., 1835, Book I, pg. 337.

(199) Ibid., pg. 317.

(200) Ibid., Book II, pg. 275.

(201) Ibid., pg. 283.

(202) Ibid., 1836, Book I, pg. 137.

(203) Ibid., Book II, pg. 171.

(204) Ibid., Book IV, pg. 153.

(205) Ibid., 1837, Book I, pg. 133.

(206) Ibid., pg. 55.

(207) Ibid., Book III, pg. 47.

(208) Ibid., Book IV, pg. 325.

(209) Ibid., 1838, Book I, pg. 329.

(210) Ibid., 1839, Book I, pg. 3.

(211) Order of the Minister of War, 16 October 1840, № 60.

(212) Ibid., 23 January 1841, № 8.

(213) Information received from the Artillery Department of the War Ministry, and a model saber confirmed by HIGHEST AUTHORITY.

(214) Order of the Minister of War, 8 April 1843, № 46.

(215) Ibid., 2 June 1843, № 78.

(216) Ibid., 2 January 1844, № 1.

(217) Ibid., 9 May 1844, № №63 and 64.

(218) Ibid., 20 May 1844, № 69.

(219) Ibid., 4 January 1845, № 1.

(220) Ibid., 4 February 1846, № 30.

(221) Ibid., 13 September 1846, № 160.

(222) Description of lower ranks' forage caps, appended to the Order of the Minister of War, 19 May 1847, № 86.

(223) Order of the Minister of War., 9 January 1848, № 8.

(224) Ibid., 9 January 1848, № 17.

(225) Ibid., 25 April 1848, № 80.

(226) Ibid., 31 May 1849, № 50.

(227) Ibid., 24 December 1849, № 133.

(228) Ibid., 30 March 1851, № 36.

(229) Ibid., 13 August 1853, № 61.

(230) Ibid., 18 February 1854, № 21.

(231) Ibid., 29 April 1854, Nº 53.
(232) Collection of Laws and Directives, 1826, Book I, pgs. 105 and 125.
(233) Ibid., Book II, pg. 47.
(234) Ibid., Book III, pg. 255.
(235) Ibid., 1827, Book I, pg. 3.
(236) Ibid., pg. 153.
(237) Ibid., Book III, pg. 89.
(238) Ibid., Book IV, pg. 267.
(239) Ibid., pg. 257.
(240) Ibid., 1828, Book I, pg. 211.
(241) Ibid., Book II, pgs. 131 et seq.
(242) Ibid., 1829, Book III, pg. 129, and information received from the Commissariat Department of the War Ministry.
(243) Collection of Laws and Directives, 1829, Book IV, pg. 107.
(244) Ibid., pg. 115.
(245) Ibid., 1830, Book I, pg. 191.
(246) Highest Order.
(247) Collection of Laws and Directives, 1830, Book III, pg. 179.
(248) Highest Order.
(249) Collection of Laws and Directives, 1831, Book II, pg. 39.
(250) Ibid., 1832, Book II, pg. 545.
(251) Ibid., 1833, Book I, pg. 419.
(252) Ibid., pg. 435.
(253) Ibid., pg. 463.
(254) Ibid., pg. 465.
(255) Papers from the Commissariat Department of the War Ministry.
(256) Information received from the Artillery Department of the War Ministry, and a model sword confirmed by HIGHEST AUTHORITY.
(257) Collection of Laws and Directives, 1834, Book III, pg. 465.
(258) Ibid., 1835, Book III, pg. 179.
(259) Ibid., 1836, Book I, pg. 137.
(260) Information received from the Commissariat Dep. of the War Ministry.
(261) Collection of Laws and Directives, 1836, Book II, pg. 171.
(262) Ibid., 1837, Book I, pg. 133.
(263) Ibid., Book III, pg. 47.
(264) Ibid., Book IV, pg. 325.
(265) Ibid., 1839, Book I, pg. 3.
(266) Ibid., pg. 179.
(267) Order of the Minister of War, 16 October 1840, Nº 60.
(268) Ibid., 23 January 1841, Nº 8.
(269) Archives of the Commissariat Department of the War Ministry, papers from 1842, Section 2, 2nd Office, Nº365.
(270) Order of the Minister of War, 8 April 1843, Nº Nº 44 and 46.
(271) Ibid., 2 June 1843, Nº 78.
(272) Ibid., 2 January 1844, Nº 1.
(273) Orders of the Minister of War, 9 May 1844, Nº Nº 63 and 64.
(274) Order of the Minister of War, 20 May 1844, Nº 69.
(275) Ibid., 9 August 1845, Nº 101.
(276) Ibid., 8 March 1847, Nº 46.
(277) Ibid., 9 January 1848, Nº 8.
(278) Ibid., 8 August 1848, Nº 149.
(279) Ibid., 19 April 1849, Nº 31.
(280) Ibid., 28 April 1849, Nº 34.
(281) Ibid., 14 September 1849, Nº 88.
(282) Orders of the Minister of War, 9 and 25 November 1849, Nº Nº 110 and 117.
(283) Order of the Minister of War, 24 December 1849, Nº 133.
(284) Ibid., 17 January 1851, Nº 7.
(285) Ibid., 21 March 1851, Nº 30.
(286) Ibid., 13 December 1851, Nº 134.
(287) Ibid., 29 October 1851, Nº 120.
(288) Ibid., 26 January 1852, Nº 15.
(289) Ibid., 3 January 1853, Nº 3.
(290) Ibid., 18 February 1854, Nº 21.
(291) Ibid., 29 April 1854, Nº 53.

(292) Ibid., 13 February 1855, Nº 28.
(293) Collection of Laws and Directives, 1826, Book I, pg. 105.
(294) Ibid., pg. 125.
(295) Ibid., Book III, pg. 344.
(296) Ibid., pg. 255.
(297) Ibid., 1827, Book I, pg. 3.
(298) Ibid., Book III, pg. 89.
(299) Information received from the Commissariat Dep. of the War Ministry.
(300) Collection of Laws and Directives, 1827, Book IV, pgs. 17 and 19.
(301) Ibid., pg. 257.
(302) Ibid., 1828, Book I, pg. 315.
(303) Ibid., pg. 131.
(304) Papers from the Commissariat Department of the War Ministry.
(305) Ibid., 1828, Book IV, pg. 57.
(306) Ibid., 1829, Book IV, pg. 19.
(307) Ibid., pg. 115.
(308) Ibid., 1833, Book I, pg. 419.
(309) Ibid., pg. 435.
(310) Ibid., pg. 465.
(311) Ibid., pg. 485.
(312) Papers from the Commissariat Department of the War Ministry.
(313) Ibid.
(314) Collection of Laws and Directives, 1834, Book II, pgs. 245-247.
(315) Ibid., Book IV, pg. 257.
(316) Ibid., 1835, Book I, pg. 337.
(317) Ibid., Book II, pg. 283.
(318) Ibid., 1836, Book I, pg. 137.
(319) Ibid., Book II, pg. 171.
(320) Ibid., Book IV, pg. 153.
(321) Ibid., 1837, Book I, pg. 133.
(322) Ibid., pg. 55.
(323) Ibid., Book III, pg. 47.
(324) Ibid., Book IV, pg. 325.
(325) Ibid., 1838, Book I, pg. 329.
(326) Ibid., 1839, Book I, pg. 3.
(327) Order of the Minister of War, 16 October 1840, Nº 60.
(328) Ibid., 23 January 1841, Nº 8.
(329) Information received from the Artillery Department of the War Ministry, and a model sword confirmed by HIGHEST AUTHORITY.
(330) Order of the Minister of War, 8 April 1843, Nº 46.
(331) Orders of the Minister of War, 10 May 1843, Nº Nº 63 and 64.
(332) Order of the Minister of War, 2 June 1843, Nº 78.
(333) Ibid., 2 January 1844, Nº 1.
(334) Orders of the Minister of War, 9 May 1844, Nº Nº 63 and 64.
(335) Order of the Minister of War, 20 May 1844, Nº 69.
(336) Ibid., 4 January 1844, Nº 1.
(337) Ibid., 9 August 1845, Nº 101.
(338) Ibid., 31 March 1846, Nº 58.
(339) Ibid., 7 August 1846, Nº 138.
(340) Ibid., 13 September 1846, Nº 160.
(341) Ibid., 31 August 1847, Nº 145, and memorandum from the Minister of War to His Imperial Highness the Commander-in-Chief of the Guards and Grenadier Corps, 5 November 1847, Nº 10,047.
(342) Memorandum from the Minister of War to His Imperial Highness the CiC. of the Guards and Grenadier Corps, 17 November 1847, Nº 10,478.
(343) Order of the Minister of War, 9 January 1848, Nº 8.
(344) Ibid., 19 January 1848, Nº 17.
(345) Ibid., 25 April 1848, Nº 80.
(346) Ibid., 5 March 1850, Nº 18.
(347) Ibid., 30 March 1851, Nº 36.
(348) Ibid., 15 April 1851, Nº 48.
(349) Ibid., 13 August 1853, Nº 61.
(350) Ibid., 18 February 1854, Nº 21.
(351) Ibid., 29 April 1854, Nº 53.

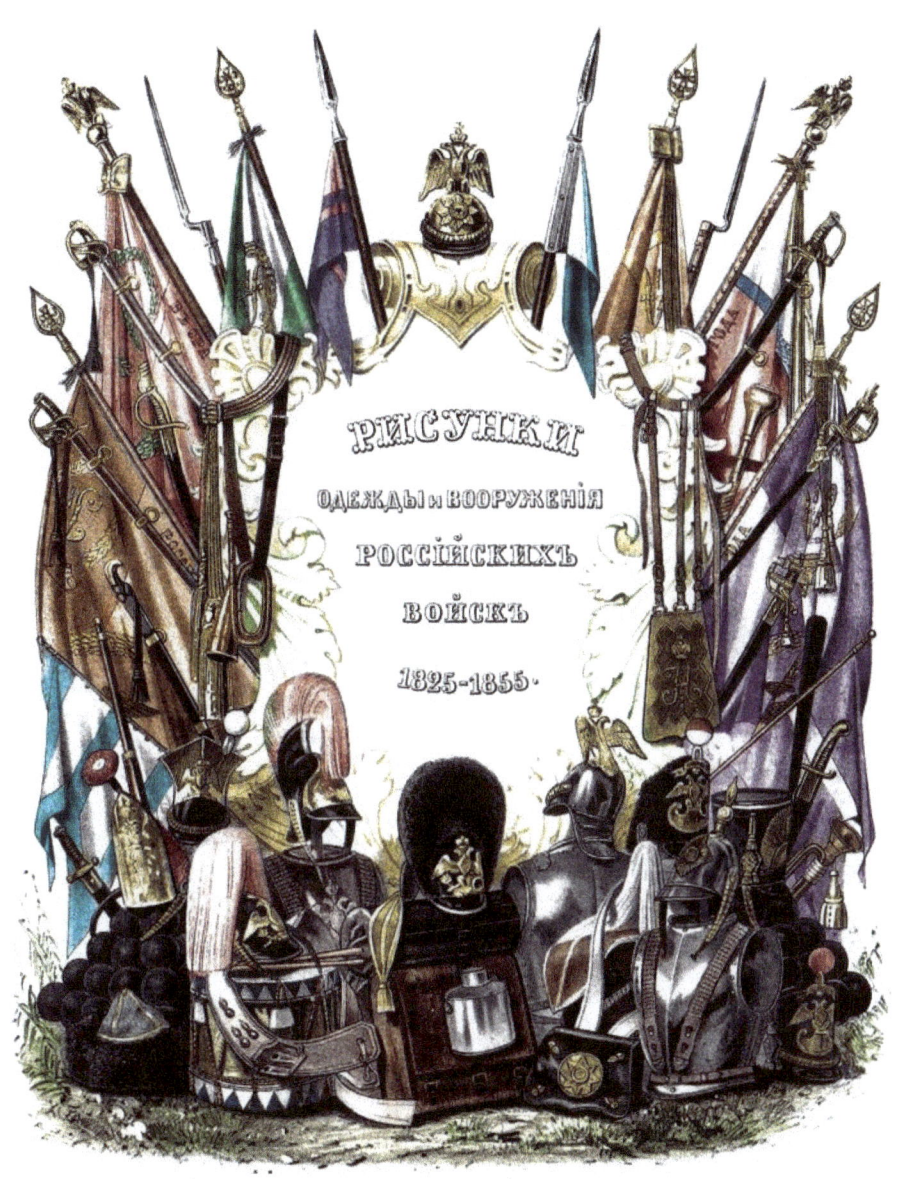

РИСУНКИ

ОДЕЖДЫ и ВООРУЖЕНІЯ

РОССІЙСКИХЪ

ВОЙСКЪ

1825-1855.

PLATES LIST OF ILLUSTRATIONS

405. Company-grade Officer. Field Artillery Brigades. 1834-1843.

406. Cannonier. Grenadier Artillery Brigades. 1834-1843.

407. Field-grade Officer. Artillery of the Separate Caucasus Corps. 1842-1848. (Note: Up to 1844, the forage cap had no cockade.)

408. Drummer. Artillery of the Separate Caucasus Corps. 1842-1848.

409. Bombardier. Grenadier Artillery Brigades. 1843 and 1844.

410. Drum-major. Grenadier Artillery Brigades. 1843 and 1844.

411. Field-grade Officer, Non-commissioned Officer Artificer, and Drummer. Grenadier Artillery Brigades. 1844-1855.

412. Cannonier and Company-grade Officer. Field Artillery Brigades. 1844-1849.

413. Field-grade Officer. Grenadier Artillery Brigades. 1845-1849.

414. Field-grade Officer. Grenadier Artillery Brigades. 1848-1855.

415. Cannonier. Artillery of the Separate Caucasus Corps. 1848-1855.

416. Company-grade Officers. Artillery of the Separate Caucasus Corps. 1848-1855.

417. Non-commissioned Officer Artificer. Grenadier Artillery Brigades. 1851-1855.

418. Drummer. Field Artillery Brigades. 1851-1855.

419. Non-commissioned Officer Artificer and Company-grade Officer. Horse Artillery. 1826-1827.

420. Bombardier and Field-grade Officer. Horse Artillery. 1826 and 1827.

421. Company-grade Officer and Cannonier. Horse Artillery. 1827 and 1828.

422. Non-commissioned Officer Artificer. Horse Artillery. 1828-1833.

423. Company-grade Officer. Horse Artillery. 1828-1833.

424. Trumpeter and Company-grade Officer. Horse Artillery. 1828-1833.

425. Non-commissioned Officer Artificer. Horse Artillery. 1834-1841.

426. Trumpeter. Horse Artillery. 1836-1841.

427. Company-grade Officer and Non-commissioned Officer Artificer. Horse Artillery. 1841-1843.

428. Bombardier. Horse Artillery. 1843-1844.

429. Company-grade Officer. Horse Artillery. 1844-1855.

430. Field-grade Officer. Horse Artillery. 1844-1849.

431. Staff-Trumpeter and Bombardier. Horse Artillery. 1844-1855.

432. Company-grade Officer. Horse Artillery. 1845-1849.

433. Field-grade Officer. Horse Artillery. 1848-1853.

434. Company-grade Officer. Horse Artillery. 1854 and 1855.

435. Field-grade Officer and Non-commissioned Officer. Sapper Battalion. 1826-1828.

436. Sapper, Miner, Pioneer NCO and Company-grade Officer. Pioneer Battalions. 1826-1828.

437. Company-grade Officer and Sapper Drummer. Lithuania Pioneer Battalion. 1826-1828.

438. Field-grade Officer. Lithuania Pioneer Battalion. 1826-1828.

439. Company-grade Officer. Sapper Battalion. 1828-1830.

440. Shako Plate for the Sapper Battalion, confirmed 24 April 1828.

441. Pioneer. Pioneer Battalions. 1828-1833.

442. Shako Plate for Pioneer Battalions, confirmed 24 April 1828.

443. Company-grade Officer and Pioneer. Caucasus Pioneer Battalion. 1829-1833. (Note: In 1830 officers' rapiers were replaced by half-sabers.)

444. Buttons for Army Sapper Battalions, confirmed 26 October 1829.

445. Company-grade Officers. Caucasus, 3rd Reserve, and Grenadier Sapper Battalions. 1830-1833.

446. Company-grade Officer and Non-commissioned Officer. Grenadier Sapper Battalion. 1833 and 1834.

447. Company-grade Officer and Bugler. Sapper Battalions. 1833-1843.

448. Company-grade Officer. Caucasus Sapper Battalion. 1833 and 1834.

449. Shako Plate for Sapper Battalions, established 5 May 1833.

450. Private. Grenadier Sapper Battalion. 1834-1843.

451. Company-grade Officer. Grenadier Sapper Battalion. 1843 and 1844.

452. Drum-major. Grenadier Sapper Battalion. 1843 and 1844.

453. Company-grade Officers. Grenadier and 1st Sapper Battalions. 1844-1849.

454. Non-commissioned Officer and Drummer. Grenadier Sapper Battalion. Private. 1st Sapper Battalion. 1844-1846.

455. Field-grade Officer. Sapper Battalions. 1845-1849.

456. Private. Grenadier Sapper Battalion. 1846-1849.

457. Non-commissioned Officer. Caucasus Sapper Battalion. 1848-1855.

458. Field-grade Officer. 3rd Reserve Sapper Battalion. 1848-1855.

459. Bugler. Grenadier Sapper Battalion. 1849-1855.

460. Private. Sapper Battalions. 1851-1855.

461. Private, NCO, and Company-grade Officer. 1st Horse-Pioneer Squadron. 1826-1827.

462. Field-grade Officer and Trumpeter. 1st Horse-Pioneer Squadron. 1827-1828.

463. Private and Company-grade Officer. 1st Horse-Pioneer Squadron. 1828.

464. Private. 1st Horse-Pioneer Squadron. 1828-1833.

465. Non-commissioned Officer. 1st Horse-Pioneer Squadron. 1833-1843.

466. Trumpeter. 1st Horse-Pioneer Squadron. 1841-1843.

467. Private. 1st Horse-Pioneer Squadron. 1843-1844.

468. Non-commissioned Officer and Trumpeter. 1st Horse-Pioneer Squadron. 1844-1849. (Note: On 28 September 1845 the 1st Horse-Pioneer Squadron was redesignated as a Battalion.)

469. Company-grade Officer. 1st Horse-Pioneer Squadron. 1844.

470. Field-grade Officer. 1st Horse-Pioneer Battalion. 1845-1849.

471. Private. 1st Horse-Pioneer Battalion. 1846-1855.

A portrait of Nicolas I. 1850s by J. Sartain after H. Vernet.

Private. Gendarme Regiment. 1826

Company-grade Officer. Gendarme Regiment. 1826

Field-grade Officer and Trumpeter. Gendarme Battalions. 1826

367

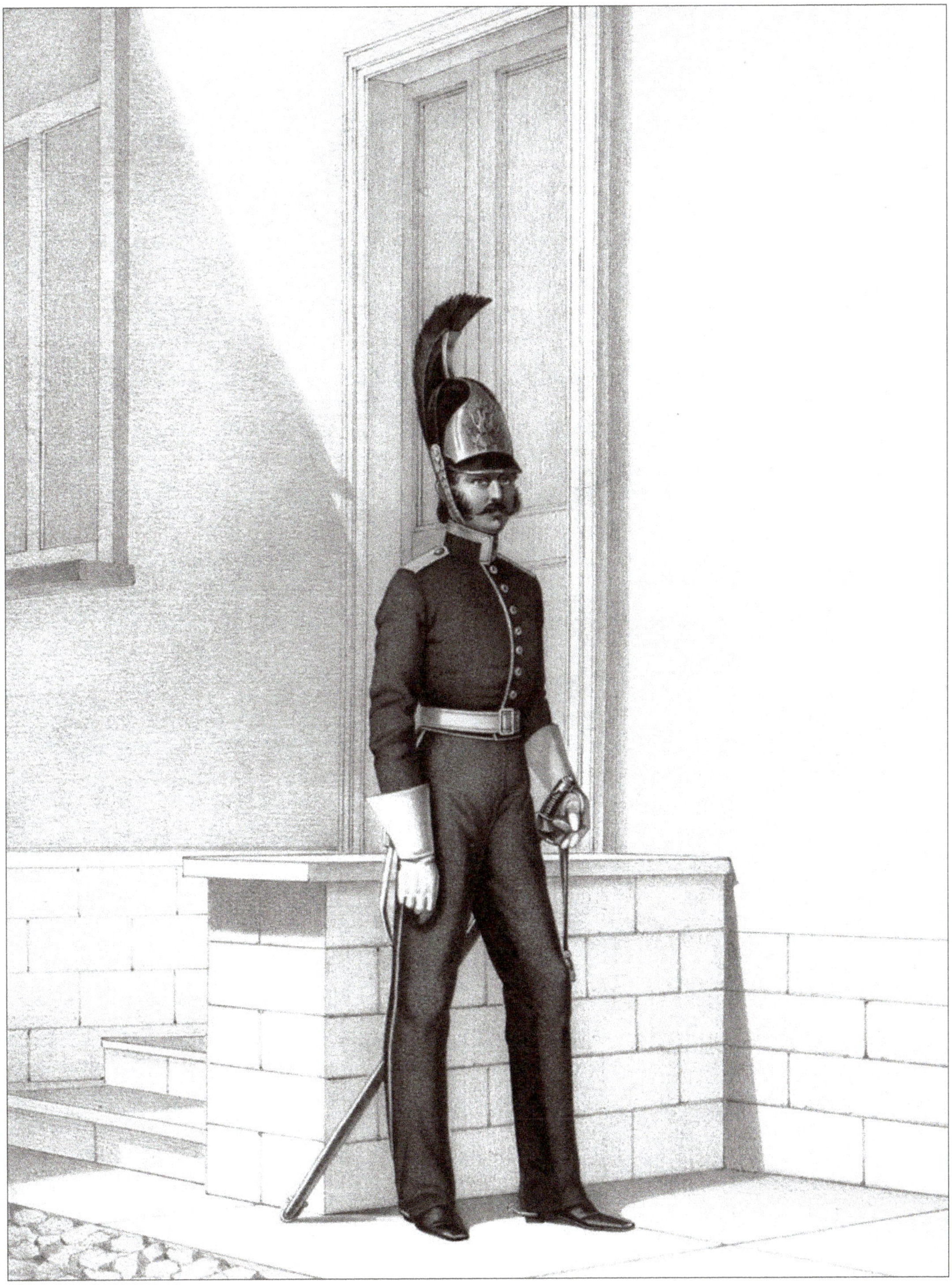

Non-commissioned Officer. Gendarme Commands. 1826

Private. Gendarme Battalions. 1826

General. Corps of Gendarmes. 1827-1845

Private. Gendarme Commands. 1836-1845

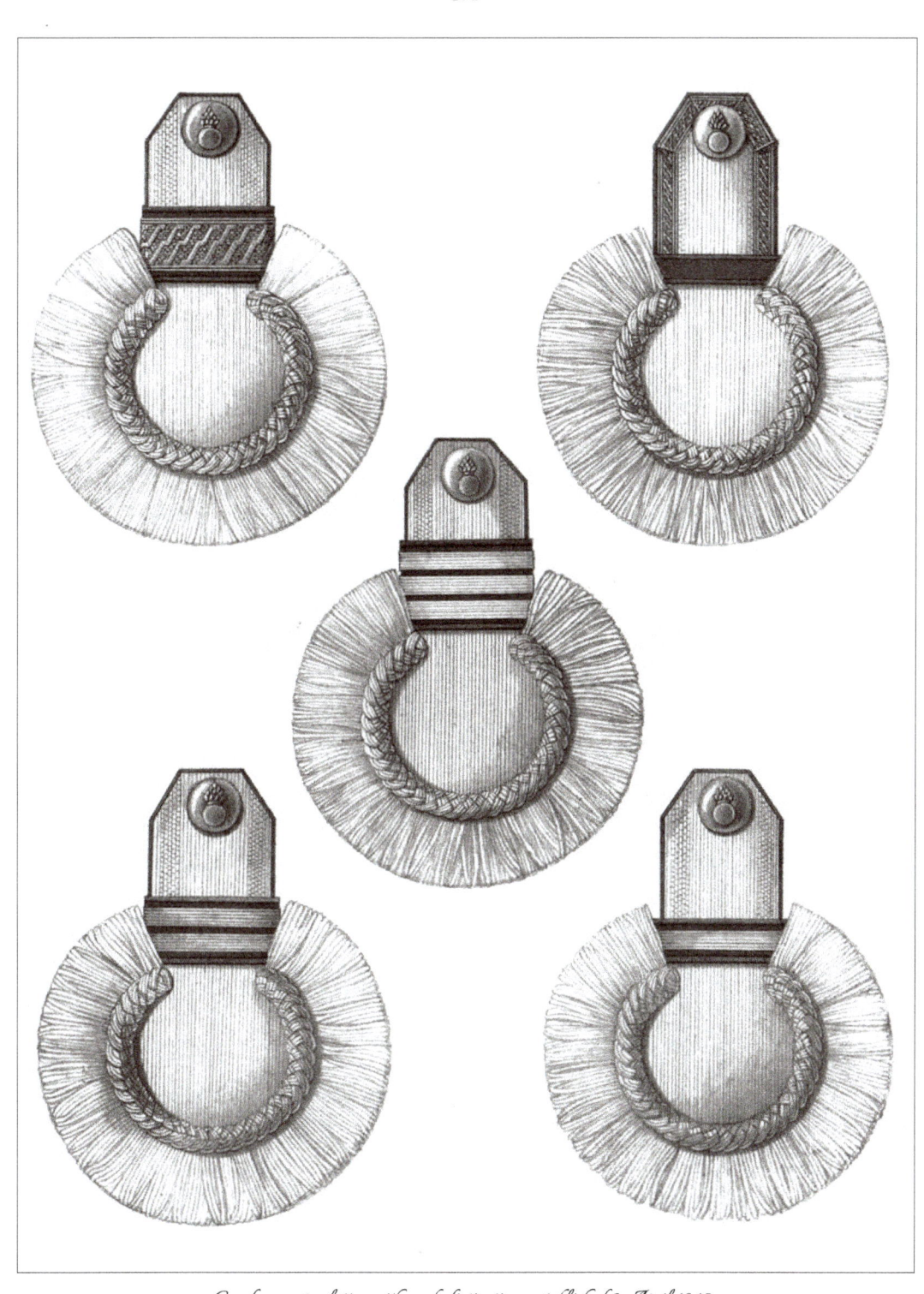

Gendarme epaulettes with rank distinctions established 8 April 1843

Private. Gendarme Regiment. Company-grade Officer. Gendarme Battalions. 1845-1855.

Trumpeter. Gendarme Battalions. 1845-1855

Non-commissioned Officer and Private. Gendarme Commands of the Caucasus Territory. 1853-1855

Company-grade Officer. Gendarme Commands of the Caucasus Territory. 1853-1855

Company-grade Officer. Corps of Gendarmes. 1854-55

Company-grade Officer and Private of the Train. 1829

Non-commissioned Officer of the Train. 1828-1843

Company-grade Officer of the Train. 1829-1843

Non-commissioned Officer of the Train. Artillery of the Caucasus Corps. 1834-1842

Private of the Train. Corps and Division Staffs. 1839-1843

Private of the Train. 1st Rifle Battalion. 1843 and 1844

Non-commissioned Officer of the Train. 1844-1849

Company-grade Officer of the Train. 1845-1849

Private of the Train. 1852-1855

Field-grade Officer and Bombardier. Grenadier Artillery Brigades. 1826-1828

Cannonier, Bombardier, and Company-grade Officer. Field Artillery Brigades. 1826-1828

Cannonier and Company-grade Officer. Artillery Brigades of the Separate Lithuania Corps. 1826-1828

Field-grade Officer. Field Artillery Brigades. 1826-1828

Cannonier. Grenadier Artillery Brigades. 1828-1833

Shako Plate for Grenadier Artillery Brigades, confirmed 24 April 1828

Company-grade Officer. Field Artillery Brigades. 1828

Shako Plate for Field Artillery Brigades, confirmed 24 April 1828

Non-combatant Non-commissioned Officer and Skilled Craftsman. Foot Artillery. From 1828 on

Field-grade Officers and Cannonier. Field Artillery Brigades. 1828-1833. (Note: In 1830 officers' rapiers were replaced by half-sabers.)

Company-grade Officer and Bombardier. Artillery Companies of the Separate Caucasus Corps. 1829-1833. (Note: In 1830 officers' rapiers were replaced by half-sabers.)

Field-grade Officer. Foot Artillery. 1829-1844

Buttons for Army Foot Artillery, confirmed 26 December 1829

Company-grade Officer. Grenadier Artillery Brigades. 1830-1833

Company-grade Officer and Bombardier. Field Artillery Brigades. 1833

Company-grade Officer and Drummer. Field Artillery Brigades. 1833

Shako Plate for Grenadier Artillery Brigades, established 5 May 1833

Shako Plate for Field Artillery Brigades, established 5 May 1833

Artillery Short-sword, confirmed 28 March 1834

Company-grade Officer. Field Artillery Brigades. 1834-1843

Cannonier. Grenadier Artillery Brigades. 1834-1843

Field-grade Officer. Artillery of the Separate Caucasus Corps. 1842-1848. (Note: Up to 1844, the forage cap had no cockade.)

Drummer. Artillery of the Separate Caucasus Corps. 1842-1848

Bombardier. Grenadier Artillery Brigades. 1843 and 1844

Drum-major. Grenadier Artillery Brigades. 1843 and 1844

Field-grade Officer, Non-commissioned Officer Artificer, and Drummer. Grenadier Artillery Brigades. 1844-1855

Cannonier and Company-grade Officer. Field Artillery Brigades. 1844-1849

Field-grade Officer. Grenadier Artillery Brigades. 1845-1849

Field-grade Officer. Grenadier Artillery Brigades. 1848-1855

Cannonier. Artillery of the Separate Caucasus Corps. 1848-1855

Company-grade Officers. Artillery of the Separate Caucasus Corps. 1848-1855

Non-commissioned Officer Artificer. Grenadier Artillery Brigades. 1851-1855

Drummer. Field Artillery Brigades. 1851-1855

Non-commissioned Officer Artificer and Company-grade Officer. Horse Artillery. 1826-1827

Bombardier and Field-grade Officer. Horse Artillery. 1826 and 1827

Company-grade Officer and Cannonier. Horse Artillery. 1827 and 1828

Company-grade Officer and Cannonier. Horse Artillery. 1827 and 1828

Company-grade Officer. Horse Artillery. 1828-1833

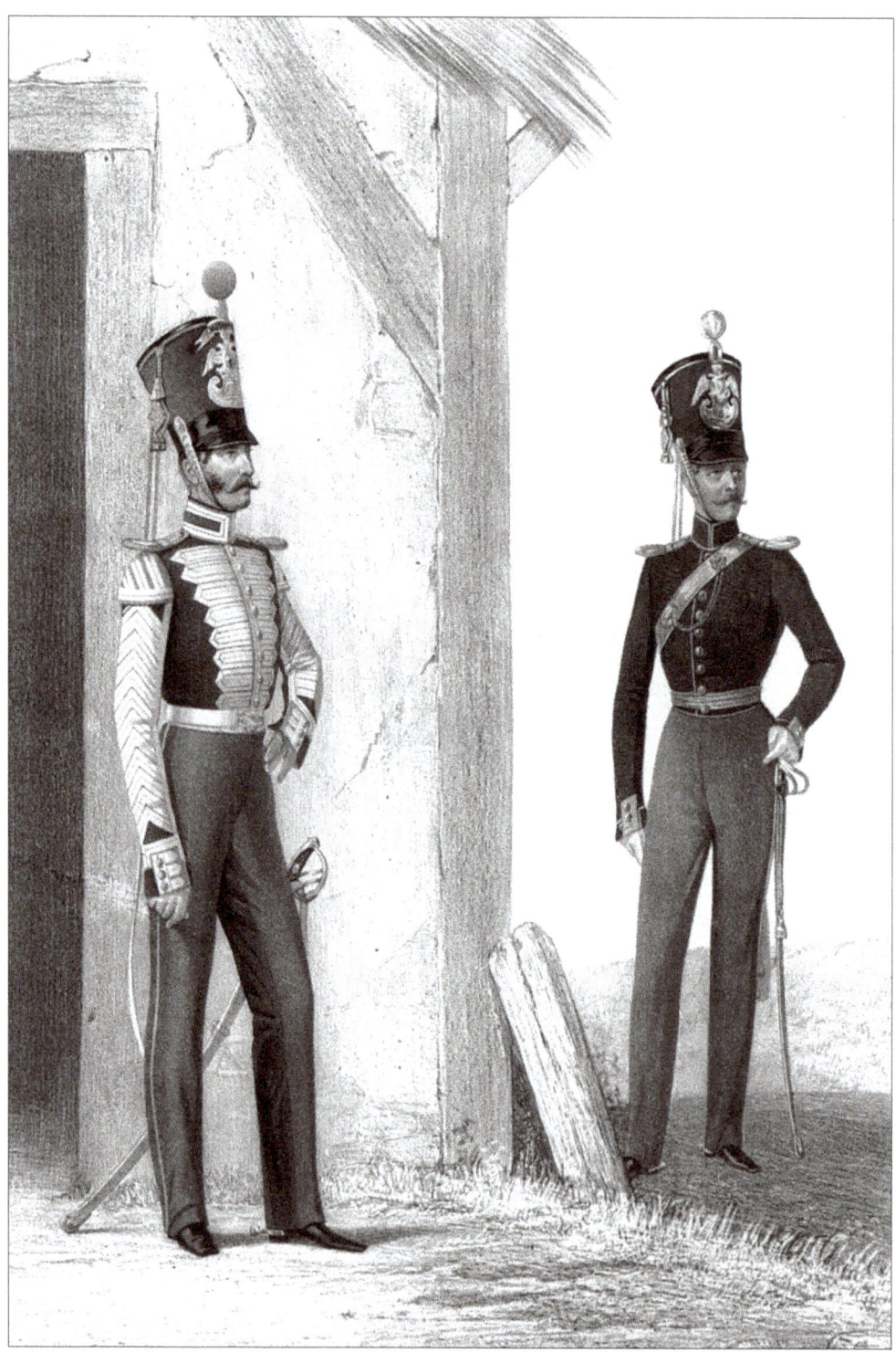

Trumpeter and Company-grade Officer. Horse Artillery. 1828-1833.

Non-commissioned Officer Artificer. Horse Artillery. 1834-1841

Trumpeter. Horse Artillery. 1836-1841

Company-grade Officer and Non-commissioned Officer Artificer. Horse Artillery. 1841-1843

Bombardier. Horse Artillery. 1843-1844

Company-grade Officer. Horse Artillery. 1844-1855

Field-grade Officer. Horse Artillery. 1844-1849

Staff-Trumpeter and Bombardier. Horse Artillery. 1844-1855

Company-grade Officer. Horse Artillery. 1845-1849

Field-grade Officer. Horse Artillery. 1848-1853

Company-grade Officer. Horse Artillery. 1854 and 1855

Field-grade Officer and Non-commissioned Officer. Sapper Battalion. 1826-1828

Sapper, Miner, Pioneer Non-commissioned Officer, and Company-grade Officer. Pioneer Battalions. 1826-1828

Company-grade Officer and Sapper Drummer. Lithuania Pioneer Battalion. 1826-1828

Field-grade Officer. Lithuania Pioneer Battalion. 1826-1828

Company-grade Officer. Sapper Battalion. 1828-1830

Shako Plate for the Sapper Battalion, confirmed 24 April 1828

Pioneer. Pioneer Battalions. 1828-1833

Shako Plate for Pioneer Battalions, confirmed 24 April 1828

Company-grade Officer and Pioneer. Caucasus Pioneer Battalion. 1829-1833. (Note: In 1830 officers' rapiers were replaced by half-sabers.)

Buttons for Army Sapper Battalions, confirmed 26 October 1829

Company-grade Officers. Caucasus, 3rd Reserve, and Grenadier Sapper Battalions. 1830-1833

Company-grade Officer and Non-commissioned Officer. Grenadier Sapper Battalion. 1833 and 1834

Company-grade Officer and Bugler. Sapper Battalions. 1833-1843

Company-grade Officer. Caucasus Sapper Battalion. 1833 and 1834

Shako Plate for Sapper Battalions, established 5 May 1833

Private. Grenadier Sapper Battalion. 1834-1843

Company-grade Officer, Grenadier Sapper Battalion, 1843 and 1844

Drum-major. Grenadier Sapper Battalion. 1843 and 1844.

Company-grade Officers. Grenadier and 1st Sapper Battalions. 1844-1849

Non-commissioned Officer and Drummer. Grenadier Sapper Battalion. Private. 1st Sapper Battalion. 1844-1846

Field-grade Officer. Sapper Battalions. 1845-1849

Private. Grenadier Sapper Battalion. 1846-1849

Non-commissioned Officer. Caucasus Sapper Battalion. 1848-1855

Field-grade Officer. 3rd Reserve Sapper Battalion. 1848-1855.

Bugler. Grenadier Sapper Battalion. 1849-1855.

Private. Sapper Battalions. 1851-1855

Private, Non-commissioned Officer, and Company-grade Officer. 1st Horse-Pioneer Squadron. 1826-1827

Field-grade Officer and Trumpeter. 1st Horse-Pioneer Squadron. 1827-1828

Private and Company-grade Officer. 1st Horse-Pioneer Squadron. 1828

Private. 1st Horse-Pioneer Squadron. 1828-1833

Non-commissioned Officer. 1st Horse-Pioneer Squadron. 1833-1843.

Trumpeter. 1st Horse-Pioneer Squadron. 1841-1843

Private. 1st Horse-Pioneer Squadron. 1843-1844

Non-commissioned Officer and Trumpeter. 1st Horse-Pioneer Squadron. 1844-1849. (Note: On 28 September 1845 the 1st Horse-Pioneer Squadron was redesignated as a Battalion.)

Company-grade Officer. 1st Horse-Pioneer Squadron. 1844

Field-grade Officer. 1st Horse-Pioneer Battalion. 1845-1849

Private. 1st Horse-Pioneer Battalion. 1846-1855

SOLDIERS, WEAPONS & UNIFORMS ALREADY PUBLISHED

(SEE WWW.SOLDIERSHOP.COM FOR ALL THE ISSUE)

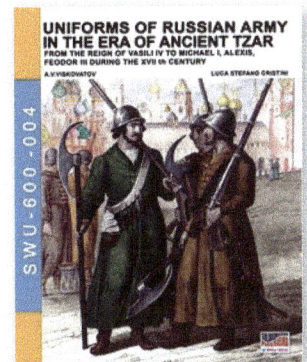

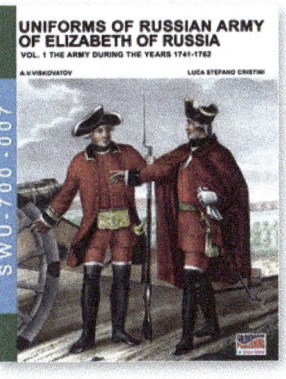
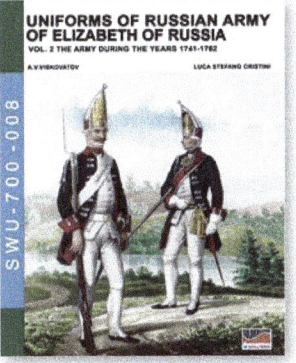

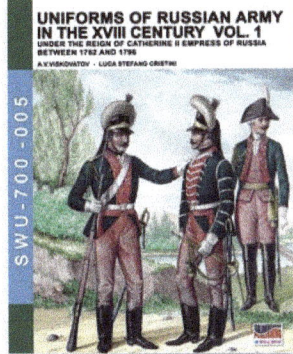
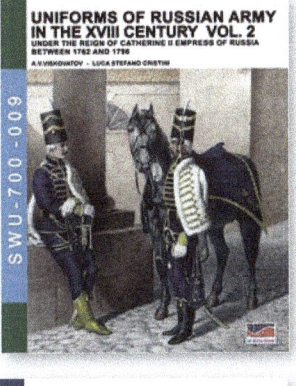
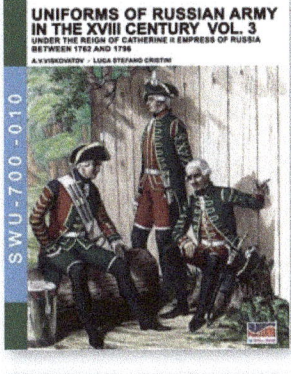
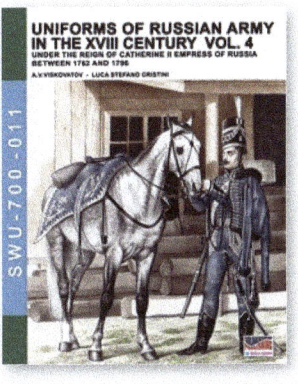

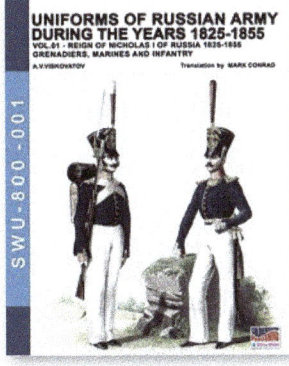

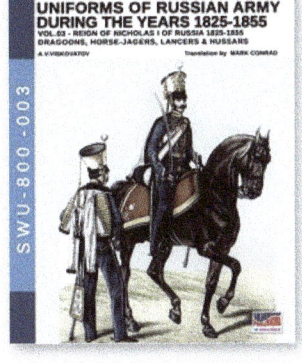

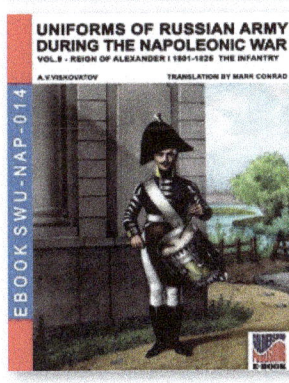

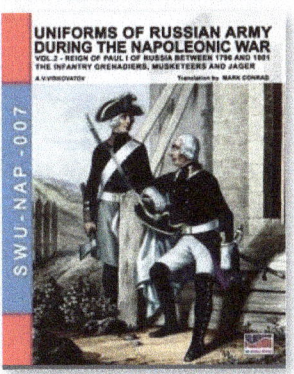